Personal Revelation

How to Recognize Promptings of the Spirit

JoAnn Hibbert Hamilton

Covenant Communications, Inc.

The author expresses gratitude to the *Ensign* for permission to reprint parts of the following articles:

"We Heard the Herald Angels Sing" by Patricia Brower
© The Church of Jesus Christ of Latter-day Saints
First published in the December 1991 *Ensign*
Used by Permission

"The Gift of a Hand" by Dora D. Flack
© The Church of Jesus Christ of Latter-day Saints
First published in the September 1991 *Ensign*
Used by Permission

Published by Covenant Communications, Inc.
American Fork, Utah

Printed in the United States of America
First Printing: February 1998

05 04 03 02 01 00 99 98   10 9 8 7 6 5 4 3 2 1

ISBN 1-57734-268-2

This book is dedicated to every person who wants
to learn to recognize the promptings of the Spirit.
May this book be a help to you
and a reminder to me, and therefore a stepping-stone
to more closely doing as God would have us do.

ACKNOWLEDGMENTS

Special thanks to the people I've learned from—
my mom, Ella Long, and my brother, Richard E. Long,
my grandparents, Elly and Charles L. Angerbauer, and other relatives who influenced me,
my Sherm and my Fred, who both showed lots of patience for me and my endeavors,
all the kids from whom I've learned so much—the Hibbert kids who refined and taught me, the Hamilton ones, and the others,
the people in the Brigham City First Ward, who taught me that there was something wonderful at church,
the members of my Bountiful ward and others I have associated with as well,
Sister DeCarma DeMars who taught me to pray,
Elder Boyd K. Packer, my first seminary teacher,
the wonderful Brazilian people,
the Brethren who supervised and helped with our mission—President Gordon B. Hinckley, President Howard W.

Hunter, Elder David B. Haight, Elder Bruce R. McConkie, Elder Loren C. Dunn, and others,

the Hill Cumorah people,

the seminary principals and teachers I've worked with,

and all those wonderful youth in my seminary and Sunday School classes.

Also, special thanks to Marilyn and Lew Kofford, who offered me the opportunity to spread my testimony in a special way; Kellene Ricks Adams and Valerie Holladay, who helped refine the original manuscript; Ryan Knowlton for his beautiful type design; and all the Covenant staff who helped and encouraged me.

Above all I thank my Father in Heaven for the opportunities He gives me, the fulness of the gospel of Jesus Christ, the benefits of the Atonement, and the knowledge I have that all of this is true.

CONTENTS

INTRODUCTION

My desire is to help members of the Church better recognize the promptings of the Holy Ghost—those quiet thoughts, those feelings of urgency, those gentle nudgings, those sharp warnings, those feelings of peace, those exulting feelings of joy, the knowledge that something is really right, and the times when words flow and ideas come that are really not yours. This book includes many spiritual experiences that are sacred and special to me. It also includes the experiences of others whom I cherish as well as experiences from General Authorities of The Church of Jesus Christ of Latter-day Saints. I have related these experiences and then given my own interpretation of how they portray the workings of the Spirit. I have also changed the names of certain individuals where I felt it would be appropriate to protect their identity.

As a foundation for this book I'd like to quote President James E. Faust, who spoke about revelation given to the Prophet Joseph Smith, as well as personal revelation given to each of us:

First, the keys and the authority of God have been given by Him to Joseph Smith and each of His successors who have been called as Presidents of the Church.

Second, those keys and authority are never to be given to another people, and those who have such authority are "known to the Church."

Third, continuing revelation and leadership for the Church come through the President of the Church, and he will never mislead the Saints.

Fourth, individual members of the Church may receive revelation for their own callings and areas of responsibility and for their own families. They may not receive spiritual instruction for those higher in authority.

Fifth, those who claim direct revelation from God for the Church outside the established order and channel of the priesthood are misguided. This also applies to any who follow them. (*Ensign,* May 1996, p. 7; emphasis added)

This book deals with this fourth fundamental truth. It attempts to help the reader understand better what President Spencer W. Kimball meant when he said,

The same revelations, visions, healings, and tongues are all available today as in any other day, providing there is the necessary faith. The Almighty is with this people. We shall have all the revelations that we shall need if we will do our duty and keep the commandments of God. *If men could just realize that there may be sound even though few ears hear it.* There are revelations even though most minds be materialistic and most hearts impenetrable. (Edward L. Kimball, ed., *The Teachings of Spencer W. Kimball* [SLC: Bookcraft, 1982], p. 454; emphasis added)

I believe that much personal revelation is just not recognized as such; it is my hope that this book will address this issue. Bishop Keith B. McMullin, Second Counselor in the Presiding Bishopric explains,

The Holy Ghost is the third member of the Godhead, sent forth by God to reveal all needful things. He teaches and testifies with divine power and clarity. His witness may go unheard or unheeded, forsaken or denied, but it is never misunderstood. . . . The Holy Ghost is a spirit personage. He has power to speak to the spirit of every man and woman, boy and girl. (*Ensign,* May 1996, p. 9)

Because there are many voices around us, it is vital that we learn to recognize the voice of God. B.H. Roberts said,

How important for the Prophet's disciples to know that not every voice heard by the spirit of man is the voice of God; that not every impression made upon the mind is an impression from a divine source. There are other influences in this God's world than divine influences. There are men-originated influences, and even satanic influences, as well as divine influences. (*A Comprehensive History of The Church of Jesus*

Christ of Latter-day Saints [SLC: Deseret News Press, 1930], p. 166)

It is how these divine influences work that this book hopes to illustrate. At the same time I recognize that each of us must learn to discern the Spirit individually, and often each of us feels the Spirit differently to some degree.

I support the Brethren in every way that I can. I love Jesus Christ, my Father in Heaven, and our living Prophet, and would do what I can to build the kingdom.

REVELATION— FOR THOSE WHO WILL HEAR

1

"Expecting the spectacular, one may not be fully alerted to the constant flow of revealed communication."

—*Spencer W. Kimball*

You are trying to make a decision about a job. Should you take it? You are considering additional education. Would it be a good choice? Is it the year to retire? What is really the best thing to do?

You hear people in church bear their testimonies and say they KNOW the Church is true. How did they move from "I believe" to "I know"? A bishop stands up in sacrament meeting and says, "I know God wants Sister Williams to be our new Relief Society president." How does he know?

These are the questions I hope to answer. I have learned that these answers and all answers are found in the scriptures. I believe with all my heart that when Noah told the people they should repent and be baptized and receive the Holy Ghost, "that [they] may have *all* things made manifest" (Moses 8:24; emphasis added), he wasn't kidding. He did not say that the Holy Ghost would help them *once in a while* when they had a serious problem. He said the Holy Ghost would help them *with all things.* This same idea is expressed in 2 Nephi 32:5 and Moroni 10:5.

What do latter-day Church leaders tell us about how God prompts and guides us? "The Spirit of God . . . will reveal to [people] even in the simplest of matters, what they shall do, by making suggestions to them," said President Lorenzo Snow. "We should try to learn the nature of this spirit, that we may understand its suggestions, and then we will always be able to do right. This is the grand privilege of every Latter-day Saint. We know that it is our right to have the manifestations of the Spirit every day in our lives" (*Conference Report,* April 1899, p. 52).

Elder Bruce R. McConkie said, "Every devoted, obedient and righteous person on earth has and does receive revelation from God" (*Mormon Doctrine* [SLC: Bookcraft, 1966], p. 644).

At the age of forty, I unexpectedly found myself a single mother with eight children under the age of sixteen, five of whom were eight and under. My husband had lost his fourteen-month battle against cancer, and I was left with the responsibility of providing for, nurturing, teaching, and supporting my children.

Only a few years after my husband and I returned from Brazil, where he had served as a mission president, Sherm was diagnosed with terminal cancer. As the cancer spread, Sherm and I talked about what I would do after his death. He was especially worried about my financial needs and pointed out that I didn't have enough insurance money to just live on it. Sherm set up a budget for me to live on after his death. I was supposed to live on $1,000 a month! With eight children! And that wasn't taking inflation into account.

"If you just spend the insurance money, you'll run out," Sherm warned me, "but if you invest wisely, it will last. Since you have a lot of health problems, you really can't work on a full-time basis and still spend the time with the children that they need."

Since he wouldn't be here to advise me about my investments, he decided that real estate was the smartest investment option. After all, he reasoned, people always need a place to live.

Sherm bought a book on real estate investment, and we tried to outline the plan for after his death. But I couldn't read the book; it was just too painful. Planning for my life without my husband was almost more than I could bear. But he read the book, marked it up, and wrote instructions in my journal.

"Don't wait too long to find a piece of property," he said. He knew me and my cautious nature all too well. "I want you to feel good about it, of course, but if you haven't found a piece of rental property within six months, just go ahead and buy something anyway. You'll run out of money if you don't actively pursue this investment program."

What Sherm and I didn't plan on was losing our home almost completely to a fire just eight days before his death. The fire destroyed fifty percent of our home, and we lost over ninety percent of our belongings. Without full coverage on our fire insurance policy, the costs of rebuilding our home were staggering. It took about eight months to rebuild our home and another seven months to replace, recover, or repair furniture and work through the depreciated value of each item that was destroyed.

In the midst of our struggle to deal with contractors and insurance agents, inflation skyrocketed. Within only a few months of Sherm's death, our tight but realistic $1,000 budget had become completely laughable. Our living expenses rose first to $1,200, then $1,500, then $1,800. As my funds slipped too quickly through my fingers, I knew I could not wait any longer to make a wise investment.

I was fairly young and totally inexperienced. I needed to find something that would provide stability and security for my large and growing family.

Only after I had rebuilt our house and settled most of the various insurance issues was I ready to take on the real estate world. I remember vividly my first phone call to a realtor. After I hung up, I cried. I didn't even know what the man had said because I didn't understand any of the real estate vocabulary that he used!

I knew I finally had to read the book Sherm had left me. By then I had a much greater appreciation for it, and I found that every note in the margins helped. I even attended a real estate seminar, hoping to learn. You see, I *could not* make a mistake. I would only manage this money once. I could not afford a bad decision—the welfare of my eight children, and my own, was at stake.

Throughout my life I have found that going to the Lord is the only real way to receive valid help. However, I understand the principle that the Lord helps those who help themselves. I knew that I was responsible to search for good property; it was up to me to learn all I could about it. I wanted to do my part so the Lord could do His.

I looked at many, many different pieces of property. I even made an offer once or twice, but then dropped the offer later because it just didn't *feel* right to me. I wanted to find the *right* piece of property.

One day my real estate agent, Barbara, and I were on our way to look at some property, and we drove past an apartment building. I looked at that building and I just *knew* those were the apartments I should buy.

"I want to buy that property," I told my agent.

She laughed, "JoAnn, it's not even for sale."

But I insisted and she humored me. We parked the car, walked up to one of the apartments, and knocked on the door. When someone answered, we asked who owned the building.

When we had the name of the property owner, Barbara and I sat down and wrote up the papers for an official offer. I figured out how much I could afford to pay, we filled out the forms, and Barbara called the man. She submitted the offer on a Friday; Saturday she called me.

"JoAnn, I'm sorry," she said, "but he turned down the offer. The property simply isn't for sale."

I hung up the phone and went to my bedroom. "Heavenly Father," I said, kneeling down beside my bed. "I know that's a good piece of property. You told me it was. I've done what I can to buy it because I really feel like you want me to have it, but the owner apparently isn't interested. Please soften this man's heart so he will sell it to me."

Meanwhile, I checked with an accountant I trust and appreciate. He said that buying this piece of property wouldn't be a complete mistake, but I could probably do better. I discussed the issue with another knowledgeable person in my ward, and he too advised against purchasing the property.

Nevertheless the feeling persisted that I should buy it, and I prayed again for help from the Lord to purchase it. I called Barbara back and told her to raise the offer $5,000. I thought that was an enormous amount at the time, but since then I've learned that, considering the property and its value, it was actually very little. But I didn't know any better.

Monday morning Barbara called. She was pleasantly surprised and excited. "He accepted the offer, JoAnn! He said he didn't feel comfortable all weekend, and as he thought about his financial situation, he had some new ideas he felt would be good for him. He said he just felt he should sell this property to you."

My hands shook as I signed the papers to finalize that deal. I didn't know that when buying real estate it's always a good idea to have an attorney look at the papers before you sign them. I didn't even show them to my accountant or to the ward member who had become a trusted financial advisor and "sounding board" since my husband's death. I simply drove down to the office of the man who owned the apartments, and bought that six-plex because I knew it was what the Lord wanted me to do.

I have a firm testimony that God heard and answered my prayers. He knows what He is doing. It was only after I forced my trembling hand to sign the papers that I learned about the man who sold me this property. Of course, God already knew this man. He had served as a bishop and knew the Lord well. The papers were fair and just for me, and God knew that, too.

During the next few years, I struggled to pay off that property so we could have some income. Ultimately, it was the rent from those apartments that put food on my family's table. It was the rent from those apartments that provided stability and security as I learned more about the real estate business, and as I took risks and got burned and tried over again. Through the years, that property has been my one piece of stable income, the one thing I can count on. I still own it today.

From this experience and many others, I know that God does know us and care about us. He will hear and answer prayers, and he will prompt and guide us.

"Get Him to the Hospital Now!"

As a "mission mom" in Brazil, I often received special help from God on behalf of our missionaries. One day the office was alerted that a sick missionary was coming in. That in itself wasn't unusual because any time missionaries were sick and didn't know how to handle it, they were to come to me.

I was standing in the entry when Elder Crump came in the door. I looked at him and saw that his companion had an arm around him. Without saying a word to either of them, I immediately turned to the mission secretary and said, "Call Dr. Anderson. Tell him we're bringing a missionary right in." I had seen many sick missionaries come to the mission home, but I had never done this before.

We got into the car and I rushed him to the hospital. The doctor told me later that had we waited, even only a few hours, before getting this young missionary to the hospital, he would have died. Elder Crump had pneumonia, and although it wasn't life-threatening, the combination of medications he had been given by two different Brazilian members had nearly proved fatal.

President Spencer W. Kimball said:

> Revelation comes to those who will hear. The Lord will not force himself upon people; and if they do not believe, they will receive no visitation. If they are content to depend upon their own limited calculations and interpretations, then, of course, the Lord will leave them to their chosen fate. . . . (Edward L. Kimball, ed., *The Teachings of Spencer W. Kimball* [SLC: Bookcraft, 1982], p. 454)

In the following chapters I will try to help identify feelings that the Lord so often uses to communicate His will to us. I will separate them as often as I can, but at times it will be obvious that, in truth, God often uses a variety of feelings in any one given situation to bring about His will.

FEELINGS

2

"Obey the inner feelings that come as promptings from the Holy Ghost."—Richard G. Scott

One brisk December day my Sunday School class had a visitor. Visitors weren't unusual, but this day stands out in my mind very clearly because it was the day of our ward Christmas program, and I had been called as the choir director about six weeks earlier. I knew nothing about leading music, but I had bought a book to show me how to do it and was determined to learn. I had already done two numbers at a stake Christmas concert, but that was the extent of my experience. Obviously, I was a bit nervous.

When I finished teaching the lesson, Susan asked to stay after class and talk. "Sister Hamilton," she said, indicating the visitor she had brought with her, "Chris has no place to go tonight." I wasn't surprised by her words since everyone in the ward knows that my family has an open-home policy. As I talked to Chris and learned why he was not living with his parents, I seriously considered inviting him into my home. He had lived with a grandparent overseas for a number of years, then had been sent back to a bad home situation, which had erupted into hospitalization, foster care, and numerous other homes. By this time he had turned eighteen and he was welcome nowhere.

I talked with Chris for four to five minutes. As we spoke I asked myself, Was I feeling turmoil as I seriously considered taking someone I didn't even know into my home, or was I feeling peace? I have learned to pay attention to feelings. I felt peace. There was no turmoil.

I excused myself and went to get my husband out of high priest meeting. My second husband, Fred, is a doll. I explained the situation to him and he said, "If you want him, you can have him."

"Come on, and meet him," I said. As I introduced Fred to Chris, I said, "We want you to come into our home, not because you need a place but because we really want you. And we want you to come in, not just as a person who is staying with us, but as a full-fledged member of the family."

I was surprised at what I said, although each morning as I say my prayers I ask God to give me the words that He wants me to say in any special situation that I encounter. I base this request on Doctrine and Covenants 100:5-6, where the Lord says, "It shall be given you in the very hour, yea, in the very moment what ye shall say." As I said these words, I realized that He was giving them to me.

I had to hurry to do the choir program, after which I would have my missionary preparation class, so I invited Chris to come to my home after that. Then I hurried into the chapel, where people were filing in for sacrament meeting. My son Dave came up to support me by singing in the choir. We happened to meet by the pulpit.

"Dave," I said, "do you see that young man there on the last bench? Do you know him?"

"I've seen him around school, but I don't know him," he said.

"Well," I said, "I feel certain that God wants him to be a part of our family."

At that, tears ran down the cheeks of my 6'8" 220-pound seventeen-year-old son. What did he feel? He felt joy and a rush of tingly feelings, and the tears flowed.

"You're right," he said.

When I finally got home after church and got Chris moved into his room, I went into my bedroom. Sometimes my best prayers are just as I walk around doing things. I remember saying, "Father, you really do want him in my home, don't you?" I felt an abundance of those little tingly feelings, those little chills, and I knew it was right (I'll discuss those tingly feelings in a later chapter).

After putting away his things, Chris came into the front room and sat on the couch.

Bonnie, one of my teenagers, said, "Hi, what's your name?"

He said, "My name is Chris."

"Where do you live?" she asked.

Hesitantly he replied, "I live . . ." he paused, ". . . here."

"Oh, welcome to the family! We're going to California tomorrow. Want to come?" was her quick reply. They talked for a few minutes before she left. Not long after, Bonnie's twin sister came into the room, and she and Chris had essentially the same conversation. The doorbell rang continually as other people involved in the California excursion arrived. There was a lot of activity as the youth gathered camping equipment from our basement. For a little while Chris wondered what he had gotten into, but he couldn't miss the warmth he felt.

I've never had someone come into our home who fit so well. God knew he would. We've sent out seventeen youth on missions, thirteen from our home. I always wanted one of them to go back to Brazil, to the country where Sherm had served as mission president and where two of our children were born. That's where the Lord sent Chris.

"It Felt Right"

Our Father in Heaven often speaks to us through feelings. "Obey the inner feelings that come as promptings from the Holy Ghost," said Elder Richard G. Scott of the Quorum of the Twelve Apostles (*Ensign*, November 1996, p. 75).

As a mission president in Brazil, my husband always approached transfers very prayerfully. He would listen to what his assistants had to say, but until it *felt* right, he didn't send out new assignments. When Sherm prayerfully decided to send one elder back to Campinas, where he had just been transferred from two weeks before, my husband's assistants responded emphatically, "But, President, we just don't do that!"

Nevertheless, my husband made the assignment, and I soon understood why. As I was opening the mission mail addressed to Sherm, I opened a letter that said, "Dear President Hibbert, I am married to a nonmember who has never been interested in the Church. I have so wanted him to join but he would never even listen. There is a missionary here in Campinas that for some reason my husband relates to. He is just starting to listen to him, but I understand he is being transferred. Could you please leave him here so he can teach my husband?"

The next letter I opened was from the same woman. It said, "Dear President Hibbert, Thank you for sending Elder Smith back to Campinas. Just as I felt he would, my husband allowed him to teach him. He is going to be baptized on Saturday. Would you like to come to dinner after the baptism?"

Both letters had arrived on the same day due to Brazil's rather faulty mail system. The Lord knew what needed to be done, and Sherm was prompted to return this elder to an area where he was able to do something no one else could.

"I HAD A FEELING"

Some of the feelings that we may experience when the Holy Ghost speaks to us are identified in the Doctrine and Covenants. These include peace (see D&C 6:23-24), knowledge (see D&C 8:2-3), and joy (see D&C 11:13-14). I have also learned that the Lord communicates with us by giving us tingly feelings, feelings of urgency, and bad feelings (see D&C 9:8-9). What I would have given to have understood this simple truth when I was younger.

In his biography Elder Boyd K. Packer tells how he was educated in the workings of the Spirit:

> Once I came to understand this [that God speaks to us through feelings], one verse in the Book of Mormon took on profound meaning and my testimony of the book became fixed. The verse had to do with Laman and Lemuel, who rebelled against Nephi. Nephi rebuked them and said: "Ye have seen an angel, and he spake unto you; yea, ye have heard his voice from time to time; and he hath spoken unto you in a still small voice, *but ye were past feeling, that ye could not feel his words*" (1 Nephi 17:45). (Lucille C. Tate, *Boyd K. Packer: A Watchman on the Tower* [SLC: Bookcraft, 1995], p. 279; emphasis added)

From Elder Packer's words, we learn that although the scriptures use the word "voice," this does not necessarily mean an *audible* voice. Sometimes these delicate, refined spiritual communications are not seen with our eyes nor heard with our ears, but rather they are *felt*. "The Holy Ghost speaks with a voice that you *feel* more than you *hear*. It is described as a 'still small voice' (see D&C 85:6). And while we speak of 'listening' to the whisperings of the Spirit, most often one describes a spiritual prompting by saying, 'I had a *feeling*'" (Elder Boyd K. Packer, "The Gift of the Holy Ghost," *Friend*, July 1995, inside front cover).

Elder Jeffrey R. Holland shared the following story in the April 1996 general conference about James and Drusilla Hendricks, which shows how the Spirit communicates in different ways with different people:

> Amidst the terrible hostilities in Missouri that would put the Prophet in Liberty Jail and see thousands of Latter-day Saints driven from their homes, Sister Drusilla Hendricks and her invalid husband, James, who had been shot by enemies of the Church in the Battle of Crooked River, arrived with their children at a hastily shaped dugout in Quincy, Illinois, to live out the spring of that harrowing year.
>
> Within two weeks the Hendricks were on the verge of starvation, having only one spoonful of sugar and a saucer full of cornmeal remaining in their possession. In the great tradition of LDS women, Drusilla made mush out of it for James and the children, thus stretching its contents as far as she could make it go. When that small offering was consumed by her famished family, she washed everything, cleaned their little dugout as thoroughly as she could, and quietly waited to die.
>
> Not long thereafter the sound of a wagon brought Drusilla to her feet. It was their neighbor Reuben Allred. He said *he had a feeling* they were out of food, so on his way into town he'd had a sack of grain ground into meal for them.

Shortly thereafter Alexander Williams arrived with two bushels of meal on his shoulder. He told Drusilla that he'd been extremely busy but the Spirit had whispered to him that "Brother Hendricks' family is suffering," so "I dropped everything and came [running]." (*Ensign*, May 1996, p. 31; emphasis added)

Notice that Brother Allred said he had a *feeling*. The family was out of food and he acted on that feeling. Brother Williams had heard the *voice* of the Spirit whispering to him that there was a need.

Feelings from God can direct and guide all areas of our lives, from temporal to spiritual, if we allow them to. God cares where we live, He cares what we do, He cares who we spend time with, and what we read and watch. He cares about all aspects of our lives.

EVEN THE LITTLE THINGS

My second husband, Fred, cares a lot about doing a good job at work. He even includes his job concerns and responsibilities in his prayers. When he was a mail carrier, he'd often have a *feeling* that he'd forgotten a piece of mail. He'd always check, and sure enough, he had. Fred explained that if he tried to ignore the feeling and go on with his route, he was always left with that extra piece of mail at the end of the day.

A young woman in my Sunday School class got a new job at a grocery store. Her first time at the cash register a young man came through the line with some beer. "I just had a feeling I should check for age identification," she said. The shopper was actually a police representative, and had that young woman not asked for identification, both she and the store owner would have had major problems. I believe God wants to help us with even the little things in our life, if we will be open to the feelings of the Spirit.

Ask and Ye Shall Receive

Please keep one thing in mind as you read this book. Many of us get caught up in focusing on our shortcomings and weaknesses, thereby assuming that we are unworthy to receive personal revelation.

If we had to be perfect to receive revelation from the Lord, no one would receive any. Investigators who have any of a variety of problems feel the Spirit during a first lesson. Members of the Church who have lost their way and are living blatant lives of unrighteousness feel prompted to return. God was not kidding when He told us to "Ask and ye shall receive" (D&C 4:7).

But I am glad we also receive the assurance from a loving God that He will give us that which is right for us, that which will help us grow and eventually return to Him. Jesus Christ said, "And whatsoever ye shall ask the Father in my name, which is right, believing that ye shall receive, behold it shall be given unto you" (3 Nephi 18:20; emphasis added). I have confidence in His choices in my behalf.

I have found that the more I listen and respond, the more revelation I receive from the Lord. I have also found a direct correlation between asking for promptings and receiving them. I am sure that obedience assists in the process of receiving personal revelation, yet I am convinced that God, who loves us just like a loving earthly parent, would help us at any time.

BAD FEELINGS   3

Bad feelings can serve as a warning.

To say that my son Steve loved basketball in high school was an understatement. He lived, breathed, and ate basketball. And he had paid the price to play it well. His team went to the state tournament when he was a senior, and Bountiful High took second that year. Steve was the high-point man in those games. He was hoping for a basketball scholarship, and our financial situation being what it was, he knew college was his responsibility.

Now Steve was only 6'6", and although that seems tall to many people, it is actually fairly short for a basketball center playing for a big college. The bigger schools look for guys who are 6'9" or 10' or 11'. And Steve wasn't quick enough to be a college guard. None of the big schools offered him a scholarship, but one small school offered him everything that he wanted—tuition, housing, and money for books and food. Best of all, he had a good chance to get a lot of playing time as well as possibly start. This college's team had done well in the nationals that year and for Steve to play with that team was a wonderful opportunity.

One day my son took our little car and drove down to see the school and accept the scholarship. When he returned, I asked him, "So did you take the scholarship?"

"Well, Mom," he said, "I had the strangest experience. I drove into the city and noticed that it was small, but I could handle that. I talked to some of the professors and the school does well academically, and I felt good about that. I talked to some of the students and felt good there. Then I met what would have been a fellow teammate, and I felt uncomfortable as I interacted with him. A short time later I went into the coach's office. And Mom, I just wasn't comfortable."

"What did you do, Steve?"

"Well, I didn't turn the scholarship down," he said, "but I didn't take it either. I just put it on hold. Why don't you drive down with me and see what you think?"

The next Friday Steve and I got in our little car, and we drove down to this college. As we walked around the campus, we felt good about the school. We talked to some professors and felt good about the academics, then talked to some students and felt good about them. Then we went into the coach's office to meet with him. As we were alone there waiting for the coach, Steve turned to me and said what I usually say to him, "What do you feel, Mom?"

"I've got a knot in the pit of my stomach, Steve," I answered.

"I don't feel good about it either," he said slowly. "I guess it just isn't right." My son turned down his dream scholarship that day. He called the coach a few days later, talked about it again, but ultimately walked away from that opportunity.

Steve played ball for Orem Community College. Because he was short of money, he tried to work and play ball and go to school. Well, his grades suffered. But the worst part of it all was that he sat on the bench. He was able to play in a few games for a little while, but most of the time he watched the other guys play.

After Steve served his mission, he played again for Orem Community College. Again, for the most part, he sat on the bench. Every once in a while he would say to me, "I wonder what would have happened if I had taken the scholarship at the other school, Mom."

Years passed. Steve married a really super young lady in the temple, and they moved to California. One time while he was home visiting, I asked him, "Did you ever get the end of the story, Steve? Did you ever find out why it was wrong to accept that scholarship?"

"Didn't I tell you, Mom?" he said. Steve told me that as the years had passed he had learned of various problems that had existed with the coach and among some of the players at that school at that time. In fact, the coach had not stayed on too long after Steve's visit. My son told me, "Because of the problems going on there, I'm glad I didn't get involved. And I think also maybe God wanted me here because I was able to influence a friend to go on a mission, and help another one to be baptized, and do some other positive things."

I am so grateful that God helped my son avoid a negative situation and also guided him to do that which was really best for him.

UNCOMFORTABLE FEELINGS

When Elder Richard G. Scott said to "obey the inner feelings that come as promptings from the Holy Ghost," he meant that we need to understand that those feelings can confirm both that which is good and wonderful or confirm that which is bad and horrible. Uncomfortable or bad feelings can serve as a warning to us and direct us just as surely as good feelings do.

The following experience shared by Brother Robert Mack Gray, Jr., is a good example of how the Spirit warns us with uncomfortable feelings:

As an unpaid counselor with my church out at the prison, I meet with large groups of inmates. Sometimes I ask my friends to please think back on the night of the crime, to think back on the time when they were on their way to do whatever it was that got them sent to prison. I ask them to show me by show of hands, if any of them remember an uneasy feeling deep in their heart. An uncomfortable nervous swelling of their breast. A still small voice deep inside whispering to please turn around, please don't do it. *Every time, every hand goes up.* Then I ask, where do you think you would be now if you would have listened? They all smile at once and say we sure would not be here. (Robert Mack Gray, Jr., *The Unseen Enemy* [SLC: Greywhale Publishing, 1989], p. 29; emphasis added.)

One way to identify these bad feelings is to remember the last time you were in a movie and a "bad" scene flashed onto the screen. What did you feel? Were you comfortable?

When I watch a movie and a "bad" scene appears, I get a knot in the pit of my stomach and I am very uncomfortable. Some youth tell me that they feel a tightening up high in their stomach. Other people say it is in their chest. One young man said his feeling was across his shoulders. It doesn't matter where it is. This is the Holy Ghost saying, "Bad scene!"

If you have seen a lot of questionable scenes on the movie screen or in your home on television, you may not have any reaction at all. That isn't because the scene isn't bad. It is because you were warned and warned and warned by the Holy Ghost that it was bad, and you ignored the warning so many times that it quit prompting you in that area. It doesn't mean the Spirit doesn't prompt you in other areas of your life, but God is well aware that you aren't listening to His directions about unrighteous television and movie offerings.

If you've become numb or past feeling, can you get the Lord to help you to recognize bad scenes again? Of course you can. Doctrine & Covenants 4:7 offers this promise: "Ask, and ye shall receive; knock, and it shall be opened unto you."

If you get on your knees and tell the Lord that you would like to clean up your mind and your actions and ask Him to give you those promptings again, He will do so. Convince God that your heart is right and He will help you. This I know.

THEY LEFT THE PARTY EARLY

So often people don't know how the Spirit works and so they ignore those feelings. One young woman told me about a young man who came to her home and asked her out. She had seen him around school and had thought he was really cute although she didn't really know him. She said, "When he entered my home, I had this knot in the pit of my stomach. I remember thinking, 'That's funny.' I thought he was good looking and he asked me to go somewhere fun, so I went and had a wonderful time. He came back the next week. I had a knot in the pit of my stomach. But we'd had a lot of fun the first time so when he asked me out again I went with him."

On the third or fourth date the young man raped this young woman. She didn't know that the knot in her stomach was the Holy Ghost warning her.

When I was speaking at BYU Education Week, a girl came up to me and said something similar had happened to her. Since she knew the young man, she ignored her bad feelings. She invited him into her apartment, and he raped her.

It is important that we learn to recognize this feeling so it can serve as the warning God intends it to be.

We don't always know the reasons why we have bad feelings. Sometimes we find out, but sometimes we don't. I know some young women who went with their high school choir on a trip to compete with other choirs in California. After the competition the young people were permitted to go to a party that was held at their hotel. These two young women were also in my Sunday School class, and they had been a part of numerous discussions about how the Lord often speaks to us through feelings. We had spent a lot of time talking about the different feelings that they should be cognizant of. At this party both girls started to have really bad feelings, and they expressed this to two other girls who were with them.

Although they had no logical reason that would justify the feelings, the four girls decided to go back to their room. When they got there they felt rather stupid. Their logic hit them, and they started to wonder why they had left a perfectly fun evening. Then one girl said, "Let's pray."

All four girls knelt beside their beds. In that prayer the young lady expressed gratitude to the Lord for removing them from a potentially bad situation. All four girls felt the Spirit very strongly.

They stayed in their room and talked that night. They never did know just why they had to leave the party. They just knew it was right and were grateful for the bad feelings that warned them to leave a possibly dangerous situation.

Learning the Hard Way

As a parent I have occasionally had a bad feeling when one of my children have come home in the evening. Usually I would talk to the child and reassure myself that there was no problem.

In one case I had a bad feeling that returned several times, and each time I allowed my logic to dismiss the feelings of concern as I reasoned about the situation. Eventually, however, I found myself dealing with a severe problem with this particular child—because I hadn't listened when the Spirit was trying to warn me to pay attention.

I have learned the hard way that the Lord is never wrong. Every time I have had a bad feeling, God has been right. He has tried so very hard to help me. I just didn't realize it at the time, and I was the loser.

I try very hard to listen to those uncomfortable feelings now. This experience added greatly to my learning how God helps us by warning us through bad and uncomfortable feelings. Sometimes I misunderstand what is a prompting and what is me—that is, which bad feeling is mine based on my very human self, and which comes from God. I am learning to identify those that come from God, and I pray that we will all seek to develop our ability to do so.

Some time after I remarried, my second husband and I had a young man living at our home who needed some help preparing for a mission. Lee had dealt with a lot of problems in his life, including extreme forms of abuse, gross neglect, negative teaching, and a lifetime of massive attacks to his self-esteem.

I had spent many long hours with Lee and had developed a great deal of love and concern for him. One day as I was driving to Salt Lake City to work on an apartment we had there, I stopped at a gas station to fill up the car. All of a sudden I had a terrible knot in my stomach and an overwhelming feeling. I *knew* that Lee was in trouble.

He had left earlier that day on a date with a friend, a woman much older than he was who apparently had different values and goals. They had planned to go hiking in the mountain, but I knew that there was a problem.

Before I even paid for my gas I climbed back in my car and bowed my head. I didn't know where Lee was, so I couldn't go "save" him. I couldn't scold him or hug him or drag him away. All I could do was pray.

"Heavenly Father, Lee has such a good heart. He is trying so very hard to get ready for this mission. He has had enough problems in his life. Please, he doesn't need any more. Wherever he is right now, make him feel so rotten, so terribly uncomfortable, that whatever situation he is in, he will just leave. Please make him feel rotten," I prayed over and over.

I paid for my gas and proceeded to Salt Lake City, pleading with the Lord the entire way to make Lee feel so very uncomfortable that he would take action and get away from whatever danger he was in. By the time I got to my apartments in Salt Lake I felt peace. Whatever had happened, whatever the problem was, it was either over or no longer a threat.

That evening I asked Lee what he'd been doing that day around 2 p.m. He responded that the two of them had been at his friend's apartment. He described the potentially compromising situation he had been in, alone with this young lady. "You know," he said, "the funniest thing happened. All of a sudden I felt so very uncomfortable that I just left."

"You Shall Feel That It Is Right"

The Lord tells us in Doctrine & Covenants 8:2 that He "will tell you in your mind and in your heart, by the Holy Ghost, which shall come upon you." This means that He will help us know what we need to know by the thoughts He puts in our minds and the feelings that accompany those thoughts. These thoughts and warnings can be accompanied by bad or uncomfortable feelings or good and joyful ones.

Let me include one more scripture that verifies that God works through feelings—good ones or bad or uncomfortable ones. In Doctrine & Covenants 9:8 the Lord told Oliver Cowdery to "study it out in your mind; then you must ask me if it be right, and if it is right I will cause that your bosom shall burn within you; therefore, you shall *feel that it is right*" (emphasis added).

In your scriptures, underneath the words "feel that it is right," I recommend that you write "or feel that it is wrong." In verse 9 the Lord goes on to say that "if it be not right you shall have no such feelings, but you shall have a stupor of thought." Notice that God is talking about feelings. A stupor of thought to me would be uncomfortable or confusing or undecided feelings.

I believe it is important to study a problem out in your own mind. It is important to make decisions and ask if they are right. Personally I think we put too much emphasis on the "burning in the bosom." I don't think I have ever experienced that feeling. Perhaps someday I shall, but I would like to emphasize that the Lord said, "You shall *feel* that it is right."

In the April 1996 general conference, Bishop Keith B. McMullin, Second Counselor in the Presiding Bishopric, said that "the Holy Ghost is the third member of the Godhead, sent forth by God to reveal all needful things" (*Ensign*, May 1996, p. 9). There are few more "needful things" in this dispensation of time than to recognize that which will harm us.

In her book *Not Without My Daughter*, Betty Mahmoody described how the Lord tried to influence her not to go to Iran, where she almost lost her daughter and her own personal freedom. She knew it was a mistake to go to Iran with her husband. She said, "Try as I might, I could not bury the dark fear that had haunted me ever since Moody's nephew Mammal Ghodsi had proposed this trip. . . . I was obsessed with a notion that my friends assured me was irrational—that once Moody brought Mahtob and me to Iran, he would try to keep us there forever."

In fact, that was exactly what happened. God had tried to warn her, but she did not understand the nature of the warning.

Betty also described her feelings when she and her daughter finally escaped Iran and reached the safety of Turkey: "Despite the incredible cold, I felt a sudden moment of delicious warmth. We were in Turkey. We were out of Iran." Betty did not understand how the Holy Ghost works by giving us feelings, but she understood what she felt, and what she felt was the Spirit telling her at an incredibly cold moment by using a "delicious warmth" that she was finally safe.

"GO HOME TODAY"

When the Holy Ghost communicates with us, we may feel a mild uneasiness or we may feel even stronger feelings, as when Steve and I visited the college he was considering and I had a knot in the pit in my stomach. In the example of the two young women who were raped, they did not know what their feelings were telling them and didn't know how to respond. As we train ourselves to listen to our feelings, however, we can identify what the feeling is. Then we can pray in a special way and take action after being warned by these uncomfortable feelings.

Early in his life, former Church President Ezra Taft Benson received a clear warning feeling and he knew how to respond. He and his cousin George were born about the same time in the same community. The two young friends joined the army as part of the World War I forces and were assigned to the Reserve Officers' Training Corps at Utah State University. When they received two weeks' furlough to return home to help harvest beets, they decided they would go home on Saturday.

When he awoke on Friday morning, the young Ezra Taft Benson had a strong spiritual impression not to wait any longer but to go home that very day. Now, if I were interpreting here I would point out that he not only had a feeling he should go home, but he also had a bad feeling about *not* going.

Ezra went home, but his cousin decided to stay until Saturday as previously planned. On that day a killer flu epidemic broke out in the camp. His cousin, whose cot was beside young Ezra's, and the man who slept on the other side, both died. Although Ezra became sick, he was home, where his father gave him a powerful priesthood blessing and his mother nursed him tenderly. President Benson felt strongly "that had he stayed back at camp with George, no doubt he, too, would have died like the others" (*Church News*, December 25, 1993, p. 7).

To Protect Another

When Sherm and I were first married we lived in Moscow, Idaho. Sherm was in law school and I taught at Moscow High School. We had moved from college housing, which was too expensive for us, to a small apartment above a furniture store. Every day we climbed three flights of stairs and trudged down a long hall to our apartment. Inside we had one room that doubled as a living room and bedroom, along with a walk-in closet and a kitchen so small that one person had to step out in order to let the other one in. The lights outside on Main Street kept the room illuminated all night, but we were cozy inside. The place was affordable, and we were grateful for it.

One night, for some unknown reason, I woke up in the middle of the night. I glanced at my husband, noticing that he was awake, and I saw sweat rolling down his face. It wasn't hot in the apartment. For some reason I whispered rather than spoke aloud, "What's the matter?"

"There's someone outside our door who wants to come in."

Most people would be nervous about an intruder coming into their apartment, but my husband's concerns were different. After Sherm's mission, he had been drafted into the Army. Wishing to take advantage of every opportunity that he could, he tried out for everything they offered. As a result he found himself in Officer Candidate School and then in Ranger Training.

Ranger Training at that time was Green Beret Training, where men are taught to sneak behind enemy lines and perform acts of sabotage. Sherm had been taught the art of killing "quietly and quickly." He had learned these skills well and was at the top of his class when it came time to graduate.

Sherm was nervous not because the intruder might come in and hurt us, but because he didn't want to hurt the intruder! We offered a quiet prayer in our bed that night. Until this time neither of us had heard the intruder outside our door, but both of us knew he was there.

A few minutes after the prayer, we both heard footsteps as the would-be intruder walked away. God helped us that night by waking us and giving us an unmistakable feeling that something was wrong and then—very likely through the use of feelings—answering our prayer by encouraging the man to leave us alone.

It is important to recognize these feelings and identify them so that the Lord with all His wisdom and judgment can guide us in our own personal lives. I'm not talking about feelings of nervousness that most of us get before we give a talk or perhaps when we have a part on a program. I'm not talking about the nervousness a young person might feel as he or she waits to go out on a first date. These feelings are all normal. The feelings we are identifying here are the "warnings," the strong bad feelings, the uncomfortable ones or the ones that indicate a "stupor of thought," that is, those thoughts of confusion that come through the Holy Ghost from a loving Heavenly Father who cares about us and wants us to be safe and happy.

KNOWING

4

"I will tell you in your mind and in your heart, by the Holy Ghost. . . ."—D&C 8:2

I can clearly remember one late summer day when as a young girl I was playing in our yard in Brigham City, Utah. It was Memorial Day, and people driving to the Brigham City cemetery often passed by our house. My grandmother had lovely peonies that usually cooperated and bloomed at that time of the year. Often people stopped to purchase the gorgeous flowers, and Grandmother gladly sold them.

On this particular day, a car stopped in front of our home and a man got out. I don't remember who else was with him. But I do remember him asking me if we had any flowers for sale.

"Yes," I answered. "We do." As we walked toward the peonies, he stopped to admire my little patch of pink carnations.

Even at that young age I *knew* there was something different about this man. I *felt* something wonderful about him. I was so impressed that, as Grandma gave him the peonies, I picked all my carnations, which were precious to me, and offered them to him.

After he left I asked my grandmother who he was. "That was Elder Ezra Taft Benson," she said.

I know that President Benson was indeed called of God because even as a young child I *felt* who and what he was. I had a feeling he was a very special person. I had actually received personal revelation; I just didn't understand at that time in my life what it was that I felt.

A few years later I had another unmistakable experience with personal revelation. Like most young women in college, I had a list of what I wanted in the young man who would someday be my eternal companion. As I dated I looked for those qualities. Eventually I started dating another student who seemed to have everything on my list. The more I dated him, the easier it was to see that he was well qualified. He was strong in the Church, he came from a strong religious family, and he had lots of ability. He excelled academically, and he related well to people. When I put his picture on my dresser, my friends saw it and said, "Cute guy!" That was nice, too. He hadn't yet served a mission but he was planning to go.

As time went on he asked me to take a priesthood pin that he had. At that time, this was one way to show a commitment between a young couple; they were then "going steady." He wanted the assurance that I would be there when he returned from his mission. I liked him well enough to take the pin, but I left it in my dresser drawer and didn't verbally commit to anything.

I had started saying my personal prayers when I was ten years old, and since that young age I had always said to my Father in Heaven, "You don't have to answer any of my other prayers if you will just tell me whom I should marry." You see, I did not want a divorce and it seemed like so many people were getting them. I felt that if God guided me, I wouldn't make a mistake.

One Saturday night I finally knelt down and said, "Heavenly Father, please tell me if this is the young man that I am to marry." I *felt* nothing, and I went to bed. At that time, I didn't know that God sometimes speaks through feelings—or the lack of them. I didn't yet understand the things that I am talking about in this book. I wish I had.

The next morning I woke up, and the first *thought* that popped into my head was, "I need to break up with him. It just isn't right."

I searched for a logical reason, but the only thing I could come up with was that he slumped sometimes when he sat on the couch. That reason was ridiculous, of course. Nevertheless, I *knew* I should break off the relationship even though I didn't realize that the Spirit had communicated with me by putting this thought in my mind.

I did break it off for three or four days. But this young man telephoned, sent a note and a small gift, and invited me to go out somewhere fun, and my resolve disappeared.

A week later I found myself back on my knees, asking the Lord the same question. Again I felt nothing, but the next morning I felt again very strongly that I should break off the relationship. And I did—for another two or three days.

Finally, the third Saturday night in a row, I petitioned the Lord with the same request. Once again I got the same result. After that, I did not pray about it any more. I dated the young man until he went on his mission, then sent him off. I didn't exactly commit to wait but I knew that he thought I would be there for him after his mission.

Six months later I sent him a "Dear John" letter. Because I didn't listen to the Spirit, I caused this young man pain that God never intended for him to go through.

I like to think that if I had known that those uncomfortable feelings I had about the relationship were God's answer, I would have followed the promptings of the Spirit. Had I understood that *knowing* the next morning I should end the relationship was my answer from God, I would have done so. Unfortunately, I did not understand at the time that Father in Heaven speaks through feelings and that when you *know* something it is often an answer to prayers.

THE RIGHT RENTERS

It was February, and I couldn't remember ever being so busy. My son was getting married, and the day after that my daughter was getting sealed to her husband. My teenage children were busy with school activities and church activities and music lessons. In addition, I had my own church responsibilities that were important to me. My days were filled with wedding preparations and chauffeuring and preparing and doing. To say I was busy was an understatement.

Just when I thought I couldn't cram one more thing into my schedule, I received a phone call. A tenant in one of our apartments had bought a house, but he had to move out *immediately.*

At the time apartments were sitting empty all over the valley. Finances were tight, and I knew I couldn't afford to let the apartment sit empty. But I didn't have time to drive down and post a "For Rent" sign, let alone show the apartment to any interested renters.

I went to my bedroom, got on my knees, and turned to the Lord. "You know and I know that I don't have time to rent that apartment right now, Heavenly Father. You also know the state of my finances. Will you please help?"

Then I stood up and just forgot about it.

On Sunday I received a phone call. A man was interested in renting my apartment. "Could you come down?" he asked

I went down, rental papers in hand.

"I'm moving here from Louisiana with my wife and children," the man explained. "I work with a crew of men, and we were all hired by a company in Salt Lake. But all of them drink and smoke, and I don't like that. I wanted to live away from them a bit.

"You know," he went on, "Utah has always interested me because I've heard that this state was full of Mormons and they don't drink or smoke."

Then he added, "I had a funny experience with this apartment. The other day I was hunting for an apartment, and as I walked down the street I just *knew* that this was the apartment I should rent. I walked by several times and had the same feeling, but there was no 'For Rent' sign posted.

"Then I noticed a young man moving out. I asked his neighbor for your phone number, and here I am. I would really like to rent the apartment."

Well, I felt the Spirit as we talked, and I rented the apartment to him that day. After he left I visited a sister who lived in the apartments who was serving as a stake missionary and told her the story. "He's just like an unbaptized Mormon," I said. Then just to make sure something happened, I called another member of the ward and asked her to make sure the missionaries knocked on the door of that apartment.

It was several weeks before I got back to that building. While I was there I saw another one of my tenants, who happened to be the Primary president.

"By the way," I said, "you really ought to fellowship that family who moved into #6. I think they might be interested in learning more about the Church."

The Primary president started to laugh. "Oh, you mean Brother Adams. He and his wife and their nine-year-old son were baptized two weeks ago. He's already serving as a den leader."

God does hear and answer prayers and through the Holy Ghost prompts and guides us. As Brother Adams walked by my apartment, he knew that was where the Lord wanted him, and within just a short time, we both found out why.

THE SPIRIT OF REVELATION

There is no doubt that God knows better than we do what is right for us, and that He is willing to give us guidance and help through the gift of the Holy Ghost. The Lord tells us in Doctrine & Covenants 8:2-3, "I will tell you in your mind and in your heart, by the Holy Ghost, which shall come upon you and which shall dwell in your heart. Now, behold, this is the spirit of revelation."

When my husband and I learned that he was dying, we spent a lot of time talking about the future. A lifetime of plans had changed as we discovered that our lifetime wasn't nearly as long as we had hoped.

During that time Sherm said to me, "Someday after I am gone a man will come to your door. He will say, 'My name is John Bellows.'"

Sherm went on to tell me what a neat man John was, how John had been a special army friend, how John's personal standards were so like his own. "I'm sorry I won't be here to see him. I always hoped he would join the Church some day," Sherm said.

"How do you know he will come?" I asked.

"He will come some day," Sherm replied. "I just *know.*"

Several years later the doorbell rang. A man and a lady stood at the door. "I am John Bellows," the man said.

"I have been waiting for you," was my reply. "Sherm said you would come."

Sometimes we just *know* something. Just as the Lord promised, we know both in our minds and in our hearts that something is true. We find ourselves saying, "I *knew* that would happen!" or "I had a *feeling* I forgot something!"

These are comments made by people who were indeed prompted. So often we don't recognize it at the time. We just think we figured things out by ourselves and got the information through our own intelligence. Although we learn much through our own efforts, the source of all knowledge is God, who relays crucial information to us through the inspiration of the Holy Ghost. So many times, when we use the words "I had a feeling" or "I knew," these words are the first clue that we've received information from God in the form of personal revelation.

When Jesus arrived at the coast of Caesarea Philippi, he asked his disciples who other men said he was. They replied that some said he was John the Baptist, others thought he was Elias, and still others claimed he was Jeremiah or one of the prophets.

He saith unto them, But whom say ye that I am?

And Simon Peter answered and said, Thou art the Christ, the Son of the living God.

And Jesus answered and said unto him, Blessed art thou, Simon Bar-jona: for *flesh and blood hath not revealed it unto thee, but my Father which is in heaven.* (Matthew 16:15-17; emphasis added)

In this scripture Christ acknowledges that Peter had not learned that He was the Christ from any man. He had learned it through personal revelation from his Father in Heaven.

The scriptures do not explain just how this personal revelation came. I personally think that it may have come to Peter just as it comes to us at times—like those times we feel something special when we listen to general conference or shake the prophet's hand. Sometimes when we hear truth being taught at church or at conference, we might feel a little tingly sensation go through our bodies. As we are bearing our testimonies of the importance of missionary work or another principle of the gospel, we may feel warmth coupled with joy, two other feelings through which the Holy Ghost communicates with us.

BEING RIGHT WITH THE LORD

We can receive spiritual knowledge regarding all aspects of our lives, from protecting our children to providing for them, from accomplishing our temporal job to fulfilling our Church callings.

President Thomas Monson once called Sherm and me into a meeting at the Church Office Building. When we arrived, there was a small group of people gathered. President Monson explained that the Brethren wanted a Gospel Doctrine manual based on *In His Steps*, a book by Charles Sheldon. We were all assigned to read the book and then, after reading and studying it, to meet again in his office at which time writing assignments for the new manual would be made. Sherm and I were thrilled with this new opportunity.

However, once we received our assignments I felt a certain amount of frustration. I wanted our lessons to be right and spent hours during the day working on them, writing and rewriting. When Sherm came home at night, we would read them through together. If we didn't feel good about one part, we would work to revise it, and we'd revise it until we felt good about it. Sometimes we'd rewrite portions of the lesson a dozen times or more.

When we thought we were done with one lesson, we would pray about it, read it again the next day and revise it again if we weren't comfortable with it. We would quit only when we *knew* it was right.

Some time after we submitted the lessons, we received a phone call. I don't remember now who called, but we were told that the five lessons that we had written went through the correlation committee unchanged. But it made sense to me that if those lessons were right within the walls of our home with the Lord, they would be right with the correlation committee. After all, we all asked for guidance from the same God.

I know of many instances where the Lord has granted knowledge where His work was concerned. When Sherm was serving as president of the Brazil Central Mission, Elder Boyd K. Packer visited the area to organize the first stake in Curitiba.

My husband told me that Elder Packer had a list of about thirty names of men to interview for the position of stake president. Elder Packer asked Sherm and his two counselors and secretary to remain in the room while the men were interviewed.

After about sixteen men had been interviewed, Elder Packer said, "I don't think we need to interview any more people. Everyone in this room knows who the new stake president should be."

He gave each of the four men a piece of paper and took one himself. "Write the name of the new stake president on the paper," he directed. Each man did so. When they compared papers, the same name was on all five papers. There was only one problem: the man whose name was on the papers was being transferred by his company out of the area.

"Shouldn't we be concerned about that?" Sherm asked.

"We don't need to be concerned about that," Elder Packer answered. "That's who the Lord wants in that position."

The next day the new stake president was sustained. On Monday he received a letter from his company informing him that the transfer had been reconsidered; company officials wanted him to stay right where he was.

"Do Not Grab the Gun"

Elder Dallin H. Oaks related a personal experience in general conference where the knowledge given to him by the Spirit had far-reaching consequences. While he and his wife were living in Chicago, they drove a sister home after an officers' meeting one August night. As was their habit while living in the city, his wife, June, locked the car door while she waited for him to walk the sister to her apartment. As Elder Oaks returned to the car, a young man came around the car with a gun, and pressed it against Elder Oaks' stomach. At first he demanded the car keys, which had been left in the car with Sister Oaks. When informed of this, the young man demanded that Elder Oaks tell her to open the car. Feeling it would be unwise to endanger his wife as well as himself, Elder Oaks refused. "Do it, or I'll kill you," the young man threatened.

Elder Oaks continued to refuse and the young man continued to threaten and make demands. Inside the car, Sister

Oaks waited and prayed. After a few minutes a peaceful feeling came over her, and she knew all would be well.

When a city bus stopped about twenty feet away, Elder Oaks began to see a possibility of help. But the passenger who stepped down from the bus scurried away, and Elder Oaks could see that the driver wasn't going to offer any assistance. The bus distracted the young man, however, who became clearly nervous. Said Elder Oaks,

> His gun wavered from my stomach until its barrel pointed slightly to my left. My arm was already partly raised, and with a quick motion I could seize the gun and struggle with him without the likelihood of being shot. I was taller and heavier than this young man, and at that time of my life was somewhat athletic. I had no doubt that I could prevail in a quick wrestling match if I could get his gun out of the contest.

> Just as I was about to make my move, I had a unique experience. I did not see anything or hear anything, but I *knew* something. I knew what would happen if I grabbed that gun. We would struggle, and I would turn the gun into that young man's chest. It would fire, and he would die. I also understood that I must not have the blood of that young man on my conscience for the rest of my life.

> I relaxed, and as the bus pulled away I followed an impulse to put my right hand on his shoulder and give him a lecture. June and I had some teenage children at that time, and giving lectures came naturally.

> "Look here," I said. "This isn't right. What you're doing just isn't right. The next car might be a policeman, and you could get killed or sent to jail for this."
>
> With the gun back in my stomach, the young robber replied by going through his demands for the third time. But this time his voice was subdued. When he offered the final threat to kill me, he didn't sound persuasive. When I refused again, he hesitated for a moment and then stuck the gun in his pocket and ran away.

Elder Oaks pondered this event many times in his life, always with gratitude, and as the years passed, with increasing awareness of its significance. Within one year of the episode, he became president of Brigham Young University. Approximately fourteen years after that August night, he was called to the Quorum of the Twelve Apostles (*Ensign*, November 1992, pp. 38-39; emphasis in original).

Had Elder Oaks chosen to rely on his own arm of flesh rather than the protection of Heavenly Father, he might have been burdened the rest of his life with the knowledge that he had taken the life of another human being. Another important principle we see here is that while the Spirit often grants us knowledge for our own protection, the Spirit also gives us knowledge to help us to prevent harm from coming to others. The experience I related in the chapter on bad feelings illustrated this same principle when Sherm and I prayed for the safety of the man outside our door.

THE FAITH OF A CHILD

One of my favorite stories showing how the Spirit grants us knowledge involves a young girl. Ten-year-old Christal Methvin and her family lived on a spacious ranch about eighty miles from

Shreveport, Louisiana. Christal rode horses and excelled in 4-H work, winning awards in the local and state fairs. One day an unusual lump was discovered on her leg. It was biopsied and found to be malignant. The doctors determined that Christal's leg had to be amputated. Little Christal responded well to the surgery, always displaying an upbeat attitude.

One day it was discovered that the cancer had spread to her lungs. At this point the Methvin family decided to bring Christal to Salt Lake City for a blessing from one of the General Authorities. Because the family did not know any of the Twelve Apostles personally, Christal's parents showed her pictures of the General Authorities and let her choose who she wanted to give her a blessing. She pointed to Elder Monson's picture.

However, Christal became too ill to make the trip to Salt Lake City. The cancer grew worse, and Christal's parents sensed that she did not have much time left. But their daughter's faith was unshaken. She knew it would soon be time for stake conference and a General Authority was always assigned to come. She did not doubt that since she could not go to Elder Monson, the Lord could send him to her.

For the weekend of the Shreveport Louisiana stake conference, Brother Monson had been assigned to El Paso, Texas. Some time before, however, President Ezra Taft Benson called him to his office and explained that another General Authority had done some preparatory work relating to the stake division in El Paso. Would Elder Monson mind if another was assigned to El Paso? Of course not. Elder Monson would willingly go wherever he was assigned. President Benson said, "Brother Monson, I feel impressed to have you visit the Shreveport Louisiana Stake." Elder Monson accepted the assignment.

In Shreveport, Elder Monson attended several meetings with both the stake presidency and the general stake leadership as well as the patriarch, and others. At one point the stake president asked Elder Monson if he would have time to give a blessing to a ten-year-old girl who had cancer. Elder Monson was willing and asked if she would be at the conference or if she was at a local hospital. When he was told that she was at home, nearly eighty miles away, he examined his meeting schedule for the rest of Saturday and Sunday morning to see if there were a few hours to spare. There were none. It was decided that the best alternative would be simply to remember Christal in the public prayers at conference.

The Methvin family was naturally disappointed, although they understood. They reasoned, however, that the Lord had brought Brother Monson to Shreveport. Could He not bring Elder Monson just a little closer so that Christal might have the desire of her heart? The family continued to pray that the Lord would open the way for Elder Monson to come to their home.

Elder Monson describes what happened after that.

> At the very moment the Methvin family knelt in prayer [that Saturday evening], the clock in the stake center showed the time to be 7:45 p.m. The leadership meeting had been inspirational. I was sorting my notes, preparing to step to the pulpit, when *I heard a voice speak to my spirit.* The message was brief, the words familiar. "Suffer the little children to come unto me, and forbid them not: for of such is the kingdom of God" (Mark 10:14). My notes became a blur. My thoughts turned to a little girl in need of a blessing. The decision was made. The meeting schedule was altered. After all, people are more important than meetings. I turned to a bishop and asked that he leave the meeting and advise the Methvins.

> The Methvin family had just arisen from their knees when the telephone rang and the message was relayed that early Sunday morning—the

Lord's day—in a spirit of fasting and prayer, we would journey to Christal's bedside.

I shall ever remember that early-morning journey to a heaven the Methvin family called home. I have been in hallowed places—even holy houses—but never have I felt more strongly the presence of the Lord than in the Methvin home. Christal looked so tiny, lying on such a large bed. The room was bright and cheerful. The sunshine from the east window filled the bedroom with light as the Lord filled our hearts with love.

The family surrounded Christal's bedside. I gazed down at a child who was too ill to rise—almost too weak to speak. Her illness had now rendered her sightless. So strong was the Spirit that I fell to my knees, took her frail hand in mine, and said simply, "Christal, I am here."

She parted her lips and whispered, "Brother Monson, I just *knew* you would come." I looked around the room. No one was standing. Each was on bended knee. A blessing was given. A faint smile crossed Christal's face. Her whispered "thank you" provided an appropriate benediction. Quietly, each filed from the room.

Four days later, on Thursday, as Church members in Shreveport joined their faith with the Methvin family and Christal's name was remembered in a special prayer to a kind and loving Heavenly Father, the pure spirit of Christal Methvin left its disease-ravaged body and entered the paradise of God. (*Inspiring Experiences That Build Faith from the Life and Ministry of Thomas S. Monson* [SLC: Deseret Book, 1994], pp. 87-90; emphasis added)

Sometimes we are given knowledge through the Spirit that will guide our actions. At other times, Heavenly Father apparently grants his children a sustaining knowledge simply to comfort us and help us to endure unto the end.

JOY
5

"I will impart unto you of my Spirit, which shall enlighten your mind, which shall fill your soul with joy."—D&C 11:13

I was attending school at Brigham Young University, and my roommate and I were eating dinner in the cafeteria. My roommate got through the line first and went ahead and found us a couple of empty seats. She took one and left the other one for me.

My empty chair happened to be right next to a tall young man who had just gotten out of the Army. I later learned that Sherm had practically worn out all his clothes before his mission. After all, he reasoned, he'd be gone for so long, he wouldn't need them anyway. He packed away his clothes, served a two-and-a-half-year mission in São Paulo, Brazil, extended it six more months, did some traveling on the way home, then returned to find he was late for his draft call. His clothes remained packed away while he served his Army time.

Five years after he left those old clothes, he put them back on to start at midterm time at BYU and, as it turned out, to meet me in the cafeteria.

Now if there were two things in Sherm's closet that did not match, he would find them. He was very forward and he talked a lot. And before I left the cafeteria he had pulled out his little black book and with no tact at all entered my name and phone number with all the others he had collected.

"That guy is going to ask me out," I told my roommate when I got to my room. I knew he would. "Should I go?"

"I wouldn't!" was her emphatic reply.

I met Sherm in November, and after Christmas I received a phone call from him inviting me to his missionary reunion. "I think I'll go," I thought. "That will be a great place to meet other nice guys."

Then Sherm mentioned that he'd heard I played the violin. "I'd love to hear you play," he said. I happened to be playing in a ward that Sunday, so Sherm invited himself along. As a result, I had two dates with this man from one phone call.

I was *not* impressed at church. Sherm had had an ingrown hair taken out just above his lip, and the doctor had told him to keep a Band-Aid on it. Still being the dutiful, obedient missionary that he was, he went through five Band-Aids that afternoon trying to keep it covered. His skin was oily, and the Band-Aid just wouldn't stay. I could hardly wait to get back to my apartment.

I wanted to break the second date, but ethically I just didn't feel right about it. Besides, this was a chance to meet a lot of other nice guys.

That night was fun. Sherm was courteous and traded me off at the dance to lots of tall guys. Every single one of them asked me, "Do you know who you're with?" And then they would tell me a wonderful story about something he'd done on his mission. By the end of the evening I was convinced that there was more than a rather forward personality and mismatched clothes to this guy.

The week before the Dorm Invitational at Helaman Halls I had a real dilemma. Another young man had invited me to go and I really wanted to. Of all the things in the world I loved to do for fun, dancing was top on the list. But I had a date with Sherm to a church seventies party in his ward. Can you imagine giving up a date to the Dorm Invitational at Helaman Halls to go to a seventies party? My dating ethics won out, however, and I grudgingly went to the seventies party with Sherm.

When Sherm and I entered the social hall at BYU, Sherm almost immediately saw something that needed to be done. He introduced me to another couple and left to help out. Then there was another need in order to keep the social running smoothly and he took care of that. I spent almost no time at all with him, but he made lots of points with me. I loved what I saw.

We dated once a week for the next few months, and finally I got down on my knees and asked God about this guy. He hadn't held my hand or kissed me, but I wondered if God thought he would be good for me. I went to bed feeling nothing, but in the morning I found myself full of joy. I knew I was going to marry Sherm, and I was wonderfully excited and happy about it.

JOY TEACHES US

In the Doctrine and Covenants we read: "Verily, verily, I say unto you, I will impart unto you of my Spirit, which shall enlighten your mind, which shall fill your soul with joy; And then shall ye know, or by this shall you know, all things whatsoever you desire of me" (D&C 11:13-14).

Elder Dallin H. Oaks of the Quorum of the Twelve Apostles said, "The Holy Ghost is the means by which God inspires and reveals his will to his children (e.g., D&C 8:2-3). The Holy Ghost bears record of the Father and of the Son. He enlightens our minds and fills us with joy. By the power of the Holy Ghost we may know the truth of all things" (*Ensign,* November 1996, p. 59). Note that Elder Oaks says that the Holy Ghost fills us with joy. The joy the Holy Ghost fills us with is one way to let us know what is right; the adversary cannot give us joy.

So, does that mean if we aren't feeling joy we aren't doing right? Not necessarily. Elder Richard G. Scott explains:

> Sadness, disappointment, severe challenge are *events* in life, not life itself. I do not minimize how hard some of these events are. They can extend over a long period of time, but they should not be allowed to become the confining center of everything you do. The Lord inspired Lehi to declare the fundamental truth, "Men are, that they might have joy." That is a conditional statement: "they *might* have joy" (2 Nephi 2:25). It is not conditional for the Lord. His intent is that each of us find joy. It will not be conditional for you as you obey the commandments, have faith in the Master, and do the things that are necessary to have joy here on earth.

> Your joy in life depends upon your trust in Heavenly Father and His holy Son, your conviction that their plan of happiness truly can bring you joy. (*Ensign,* May 1996, p. 24)

Joy, then, is one of the results of doing right, and so when we feel joy, we can be assured that our actions have been correct.

Like most other emotions, joy is felt in different degrees and in different ways. Sometimes joy totally fills our being and we feel absolutely wonderful. Other times it is a warm, satisfied feeling, or perhaps it is somewhere between these two perimeters.

Two of my seminary students—a young lady and a young man—were astounded at the joy they felt when they left a compromising situation. They had two of the four leads in a school play. Rehearsal had been going well, and the play was just four weeks away. One day they came to class and said that the night before, the cast had gone through the second act. They were shocked at what they were expected to do, and they didn't feel comfortable with what they had to say. Realizing that they wouldn't want their parents or seminary teacher to come to the play, they wondered what they should do.

"Let's use my daughter's test for honesty and integrity," I said. "First, if it bothers you, it's wrong. Second, if you wouldn't do it if Christ or your parents were there, it's wrong. And third, if you have to rationalize, it's wrong. What do you think?"

As a class we talked about the problem and about the feelings involved. These two students knew that people would be upset and angry at them if they withdrew from the play.

Nevertheless, that night they and several other students dropped out of the play. Much to their surprise, they felt "wonderful" after they did so. Their feelings told them they had done the right thing. The young lady who had given up one of the leads was amazed at how good she felt. She said to me, "If I'd stayed in the play, I would have missed these wonderful feelings."

The joy my students felt at leaving a compromising situation was the Spirit telling them they had made the right decision.

FRUITS OF THE SPIRIT

In the spring an apple tree has blossoms, which, after a period of time, fall to the ground leaving buds that grow and eventually develop into apples. The fruit of the tree is the apple. Galatians 5:22-23 tells us about the fruits of the Spirit, which are "love, *joy*, peace, longsuffering, gentleness, goodness, faith, meekness, temperance."

Often we haven't been taught or simply don't realize that feelings of joy can be personal revelation from Heavenly Father. While we were in Brazil sometimes young missionaries would say to me, "I'm not having any spiritual experiences. I'm doing my best and I've been here four months and I'm just not having any spiritual experiences."

It was so fun to sit down with them and say, "Elder, when did you last teach a first lesson?"

"Yesterday," was the quick reply.

"Did you tell the Joseph Smith story in the first lesson?"

"Yes."

"How did you feel?"

"Oh, I feel so wonderful when I tell the Joseph Smith story. I feel WONDERFUL!"

And then I'd say to the young missionary: "Do you realize that the joy you feel and those wonderful feelings that you have when you tell the Joseph Smith story are the Holy Ghost bearing testimony to you that what you are saying is true? That is indeed personal revelation to you and a special spiritual experience."

When I was in charge of the missionary preparation program at the LDS Business College, the class and I would go proselyting with the full-time missionaries. One night our group of about 200 youth headed out, partnered with the missionaries in the area. We also had returned missionaries supervising small groups of youth since we didn't have enough full-time missionaries to do splits with.

I stayed at the college to hear the result of the evening from the young people and to collect the referrals that they gathered. As one young man climbed the stairs and rounded the corner to where I could see him, it was easy to sense the *joy* he was feeling. His face simply glowed. The smile was bigger than I had ever seen it and his eyes just shone.

"Tell me what happened," I asked.

"Oh Sister Hamilton, wait till you hear what happened to me. We went up to this door, and this guy answered it. He was smoking, and he wasn't even listening to me, but I bore testimony of Joseph Smith and I felt the Spirit for the first time in my life. The Church is true, Sister Hamilton!" Through joy, and perhaps other feelings as well, the Spirit had testified to this young man.

Another young man came to my house to tell me that his missionary papers were going to go in on Sunday. You should have seen his eyes. You should have seen the size of his smile. You should have felt the joy that he felt. I felt it, too. The Holy Ghost was saying, "That's wonderful!" The Adversary can't give us feelings like that.

"A SPIRIT OF PURE JOY"

When ward members were asked to offer service to unwed mothers as foster parents, April Goodman Baird responded willingly. "The Spirit [spoke] to me, and I felt very strongly that this was a service in which the Lord wanted my family to be involved," she said. When the first unwed mother came to stay in their home, the Baird family received a witness of the Spirit that this eighteen-year-old mother was to be their first foster daughter.

During the young mother's stay with the Bairds, April said "we felt both *joy* and sorrow. It was a glorious experience full of love and learning, and a bond was formed between Jill and our family that will never be broken" (emphasis added).

When April was asked to pick up a newborn baby from the hospital, she quietly watched the tender farewell between the young mother and the baby she was giving up for adoption.

> [The young mother] was sitting on the edge of
> her hospital bed, cradling in her arms a beautiful
> baby girl, a gift from God. Her mother and father
> were standing arm in arm, looking out the
> window . . . trying to keep their composure and
> be strong for their daughter. I was very nervous

about entering that room and intruding on the spirit that was there. I felt as if I might be stepping on hallowed ground.

The new mother was cooing to her daughter, expressing her deep love for her, telling her she was going to have some great opportunities in life by going to an adoptive family—opportunities she might not have otherwise. She whispered that she would never forget her and that someday, if the Lord permitted, they might have a chance to meet again. Her final words to her infant daughter were, "If I didn't love you with ever fiber of my soul, if I didn't know beyond any doubt that you were to belong to another family, I would never let you go!" She kissed the tiny forehead and pressed her lips against each infant finger. Then she passed her baby from her aching arms to mine, turned away, and broke into sobs. Her mother and father cried with her and encircled her in their arms as I left with the baby.

I cried all the way home for that precious little mother. . . .

April served as a foster parent to the small infant for just two days while the adoptive parents were notified. When they came to pick up their new baby, April went to meet them. She said she "entered [the] room filled with a mighty spirit, but this time a spirit of *pure joy*. The cycle was complete as the baby was passed from my arms to the aching arms of her new mother. Tears flowed down the new parents' cheeks, and I left the room quietly. Like them, I too was shedding tears of joy!"

Through feelings of joy, April felt the confirmation of the Spirit that she was a part of a holy service ("Aching Arms," in

Michele Garvin, ed., *By Small and Simple Means*, Covenant
Communications, 1996, pp. 21-23; emphasis added).

WILLING SERVICE IS KEY

The joys we are discussing here do not result from the
pursuit of pleasure or fun. As Elder Scott has said, "You are here
on earth for a divine purpose. It is not to be endlessly entertained
or to be constantly in full pursuit of pleasure. You are here to be
tried, to prove yourself so that you can receive the additional
blessings God has for you" (*Ensign,* May 1996, p. 25). When we
are doing as He would have us do, at times He lets us know that
we are right on track by giving us a wonderful burst of joy.

Elder Scott continued: "When you trust in the Lord, when
you are willing to let your heart and your mind be centered in His
will, when you ask to be led by the Spirit to do His will, *you are
assured of the greatest happiness* along the way and the most fulfilling
attainment from this mortal experience" (ibid.; emphasis added).
Elder Scott suggested that willing service is a key to enduring happiness, and he told of a woman who was joyously happy. "Each
morning she would ask her Father in Heaven to lead her to someone
she could help," he said. "That sincere prayer was answered time and
again. The burdens of many were eased and their lives brightened.
She was blessed continually for being an instrument directed by the
Lord." And how was she blessed? "By receiving a dose of joy over
and over to confirm the rightness of her actions."

When we do God's will, and especially when we ask to be
led by the Spirit, we receive happiness along the way. Happiness
is a feeling, and Father in Heaven lets us know that He is
pleased through these feelings. They do not necessarily come
when we choose to have them. They come when God chooses to
put His stamp of approval on an action and possibly an attitude.
These are real feelings given to us from God.

Often when I leave a salad with someone who needs it, I
feel joy as I walk away. I have a happy feeling and I know in my
heart that I did right.

We can feel the same way as we walk away from a gospel-oriented discussion where we testified of truth. We can feel it as we leave a Sub-for-Santa project or the community hospital or even just a visiting teaching appointment. So often this feeling of joy includes elation and happiness. Sometimes I want to shout to the world about how great I feel as I come out of a Sunday School class or a seminary class where I felt the Spirit and I know the youth did as well.

I have experienced this feeling as I bought cans for food storage. As we have opened our home to others in need, God has let us know through that feeling of joy that we are doing His work. The payback for service that He wants done is far greater than any service rendered. You cannot get ahead of the Lord, only farther in debt to Him.

When Jesus Christ was telling the parable of the talents, he concluded with the servant who had doubled his five talents by saying: "His lord said unto him, Well done, thou good and faithful servant: thou hast been faithful over a few things, I will make thee ruler over many things: enter thou into the joy of thy lord" (Matthew 25:21). The same response was given to the servant who doubled his gift of two talents. Those servants had pleased their Lord and, consequently, received great joy.

I believe we can have no greater objective than to obtain this same joy, the joy that is ours when we obey our Lord and Master, when we reach out in service and love to others, when we strive to be worthy of our Father's presence, and when we promptly obey all personal revelation He gives us to guide and protect us in this mortal probation.

PEACE AND COMFORT

6

"Did I not speak peace to your mind concerning the matter? What greater witness can you have than from God?"—D&C 6:23

I was at home when I received the phone call no mother wants to ever receive: one of my children was in danger. My older son had gone to Snow Basin snowmobiling with a date. He was calling me on his cellular phone to let me know his situation. He was lost somewhere in the mountains, his snowmobile had slipped in a ravine and the belt had come off, he had a replacement belt but didn't know how to put it on, he had no idea where his date was, and the batteries were running low on his phone.

Frantically we called the woman he had rented the snowmobiles from; he'd already alerted her of the problem. She, in turn, had notified the Snow Basin Search and Rescue Team as well as numerous other people in the area. Dozens of experienced people were combing the area, looking for my son and his date as fog settled in and visibility was reduced to less than ten feet.

After getting off the phone, we knelt in prayer, asking God to help the search and rescue team find my son. Following the prayer, I continued to worry, but my teenage son Dave appeared unconcerned. "Don't worry, Mom," he said. "Dale will be all right. Don't you feel the peace?" Then he and his friends went on with what they were doing.

However, I remained concerned. From time to time I called the rescue operations to see if there was any progress, bothering them and worrying myself although in my heart I truly did feel that Dale would be fine.

Eventually we received word that Dale's date had been found. She had headed up the hill in a different direction, and her snowmobile had gotten stuck in the snow, too. Search and rescue team members found her trudging down the mountain.

Even though Dale had not been located, there was a feeling of peace in our home. Two hours later, my son was found, uninjured even though he had spent hours in the winter mountains.

"See, Mom," his younger brother commented. "The Lord knew all along that Dale was fine and that there would be no problem."

AN ASSURANCE THAT CANNOT COME FROM MAN

Elder John Taylor said, "Peace is the gift of God. Do you want peace? Go to God. Do you want peace in your families? Go to God. Do you want peace to brood over your families? If you do, live your religion, and the very peace of God will dwell and abide with you, for that is where peace comes from, and it doesn't dwell anywhere else" (Rulon T. Burton, *We Believe— Doctrines and Principles of The Church of Jesus Christ of Latter-day Saint* [SLC: Tabernacle Books, 1994], p. 631).

Peace is felt on numerous occasions; it can come to us in a loud, crowded room or when we are on our knees in the dark of the night, whether we're looking for assurance that a decision we've made is right or whether we're worried about a child who is lost or ill. It is one of the most glorious ways that the Lord communicates with us because, if we heed it, this gentle communication brings an end to our turmoil, indecision, and fear.

Elder Gene R. Cook shares a personal experience when peace reassured him in a situation where tremendous concern and worry would have been the natural reaction:

> When I was a mission president, a missionary once called the mission home about 2:00 a.m. saying his companion had left for the evening with a local companion and had never come home. My assistants drove to my home to inform me; when I got word, I immediately called the missionary and asked if there had been any problems the night before. He said no. I asked if his companion had been in a good mood before he left to proselyte that night. He said yes.
>
> I thanked him, hung up the phone, and then knelt in my living room with my two assistants and offered prayer. As I prayed, I had the assurance that Elder Jones was all right and *that we needn't worry.* (I didn't have any idea where he was or when he would return, but *I knew* he was okay.) After we prayed, the assistants wanted to know what they should do next. I said, "I think you should go home and get some sleep. Remember, at 9:00 a.m. we're scheduled to travel to Paraguay." One of them asked me, "Do you mean we will go even if Elder Jones has not returned yet?" and I said, "No, he will be back. Just exercise faith and he will be back."

By 8:30 the next morning, Elder Jones still had not returned. The assistants and I were in the assistants' office. We prayed again and told the Lord that we had some very important things to do in Paraguay, and we wanted to know what to do. *I felt the same thing* I had felt the night before. "Don't worry about it; he will return before you leave." We stood from that prayer and I told my assistants, "Brethren, let's not worry about it. He'll be back in time."

About ten minutes before nine, when we had our bags packed and were ready to leave, Elder Jones arrived at the door of the mission home. Of course we were all relieved to see him. I immediately took him into the office to interview him about where he'd been and what he'd been doing the whole night. It turned out that in his great zealousness to preach the gospel he and his local companion had gone to a neighboring town where no missionaries were assigned. He had gone into the home of a member family, had organized a group of people to teach, and had preached to them late into the night. It had not even crossed his mind that his companion would be worried about him. He had come in to the mission home, quite excited, to suggest that I open up a new city and place missionaries there.

After expressing his gratitude for the peace he felt in answer to his prayer, Elder Cook said, "I bear testimony that the feeling of peace and assurance I had cannot come from men; it comes from the Lord. It enables you to go ahead with your task or your life with assurance—even though you're short on facts—

that everything will work out all right (Gene R. Cook, *Receiving Answers to Our Prayers* [SLC: Deseret Book, 1996], pp. 80-81; emphasis added).

"SOMEONE OUT HERE NEEDED HELP"

The Holy Ghost "has the power to give peace to the soul of the righteous," stated Elder Delbert L. Stapley (*Conference Report*, October 1996, pp. 113-14). This feeling confirms rightness of an action as well as a state of living. Galatians 5:22 verifies that this peace is the "fruit of the Spirit," or in other words, the result of doing things of the Spirit. Stories abound that remind us that the Lord watches over us and sends help to us in moments of great need. Often as we seek His loving care and guidance in these desperate moments, we are comforted with feelings of peace.

John Morgan, a former Southern States mission president, tells this story about two of his elders. He had directed them to start on their journey by foot to a hitherto unvisited section of the country and to travel without purse or script. As the evening fell, it began to rain. There was no shelter in sight. The storm grew in its intensity, and the two elders sought refuge under some trees.

> The rain rapidly developed into a torrent and the Elders were soon drenched to the skin. It grew desperately dark. The trail through the trees was a heavy one; sticky clay made it most difficult to travel. Tired, hungry and cold, they stopped to rest. The rain had ceased, but they did not know where they were or what to do. In that moment, Elder Ford's companion, trembling with cold and emotion, suggested that they kneel on the damp ground and pray; that President Morgan had promised them divine aid should circumstance require it.

Surely they had done their duty and were willing and desirous of carrying on. Surely, God would hear and answer their prayer. Then on bended knees, far from home and loved ones, lost in what they thought was wholly uninhabited country in the cold and dampness of the woods, the two young Elders knelt in prayer. Elder Ford did the praying. He had prayed daily since he was a boy at his mother's knee, but never until now had he known the true meaning and power of prayer. He . . . pleaded for the help necessary to assist them out of their miserable dilemma; and as he prayed, they felt a divine influence about them and in that moment of supplication they received assurance that the Lord would help them to security and peace of mind. In closing his prayer, Elder Ford in deep humility, thanked their Heavenly Father for His blessings and for His Spirit which had enlightened their minds and assured them the security for which they prayed.

They arose to their feet and scarcely had risen when they heard measured footbeats as though a horse was approaching; then through the darkness of the night, they saw the flickering light of a lantern through the trees and they knew that someone was approaching.

The man who found them said, "I went to bed pretty tired tonight and I just couldn't sleep. I tossed and turned in bed with a constantly growing feeling that someone out here needed help. I don't know why I did it, but I got out of a nice warm bed and came out into the rain and cold and through these woods because I felt that someone was in trouble. I guess it was you boys who just wouldn't let me go to sleep." (Bryant S. Hinckley, *The Faith of Our Pioneer Fathers* [SLC: Deseret Book, 1956], pp. 252-55)

This man asked them why they were there and then took them to his home. Before they woke the next day, he had gone to the homes of his friends and neighbors and invited them to come to his home that evening to listen to these young missionaries. The meeting was held and then another and another. Soon one family and then another sought baptism until most of the people in the valley were baptized as members of the Church.

"ALL I HAD TO DO WAS ENDURE"

Opposition often comes, even after we've received peace and revelation. But we must remember we've already received our answer from the Lord. Exercising faith in that answer of peace is our challenge.

"A few years ago I was injured in an accident and spent some time recovering," recalled Marjean Kamerath. "I was just starting to feel better when there were some further complications from the injury, and I was bedridden for what seemed to me a very long time. I read the scriptures daily and prayed that I might recover quickly. I felt peace and comfort in my heart, and knew that I would be made whole. It just seemed to be such a long process" ("Living by the Scriptures," *Church News,* January 11, 1997). Those long processes are refining periods that prepare us even better to receive revelation from the Lord and to be an instrument in His hands.

These feelings of peace, these confirmations of Heavenly Father's love can make enduring a little easier, however. Knowing in our hearts and minds that a loving Father is aware of us, that He knows us and loves us, can make terrible moments or days or weeks or months or years a tiny bit sweeter. These brief moments of peace can help us hold on just a bit longer.

One brother, Lee Christensen, told how after his father's death, it fell to him to care for the small farm. At the time Brother Christensen was commuting over 120 miles to work daily, he was serving in a bishopric even as he was still finishing his education. He felt that "[his] days dragged on in a seemingly never-ending cycle of heavy responsibilities to be shouldered in the cold and wet weather." One freezing February morning, Brother Christensen arose at 4:00 a.m. to care for the stock before he went to work.

> The cattle to be fed were some distance from our home, but because of the excessive snowfall and poor visibility, I trudged through the snow in a drain ditch to avoid cars on the road. Sloshing through mud and broken ice, I stumbled several times, so that by the time I arrived at the feedlot I was soaked from head to toe, splattered with mud, my clothes frozen stiff. I was already late because of the walk, so I had to hurry or miss my ride to work.

Although Lee pushed and pulled at the gate of the feedlot, it refused to budge. It was completely frozen shut. "After beating, prying, pushing, and pulling at it, I knew I was defeated," Lee continued. "I didn't have time to walk back to the house, yet the cattle had to be fed. *I can't go on*, I thought. *I just can't do it all any longer.*"

Standing there, considering the cold, hungry animals, Lee had a sudden mental picture of his father, who had faced similar struggles for many years. Lee then remembered other pioneer ancestors and thought of the challenges they had had to overcome. Feeling inferior to his father and ancestors, Lee questioned whether he would ever be worthy of them. He said:

> I fell to my knees, and there in the slush I tearfully asked to be forgiven for my weakness and

pleaded for help from my Father in Heaven to continue doing what was necessary for my family.

As I prayed, a sweet, calming peace entered me. I knew I was loved and appreciated and that all I had to do was to endure.

I stood up quietly and walked to the frozen gate. With one small tug, it swung open. My prayer had been heard. I knew then that Father in Heaven loved me and that a way would be provided for me to carry on with all my responsibilities. ("The Gate," *Ensign*, February 1996, pp. 60-61)

SACRED SITES WHERE PEACE CAN BE FOUND

Going to the temple to do baptisms for the dead or even endowment work can be a lot of fun. But it is possible to be so involved with the friends we go to the temple with that we feel only the enjoyment of being with friends or family.

However, when we enter the temple of the Lord with the right spirit, we might feel a wave of peace surround us simply by entering the building. We might even feel this peace at any location inside the building, depending on where our minds and hearts are. As we do the work in the house of the Lord and communicate with Him, in our minds we may feel little chills or tingles, and we almost always feel joy and peace. It is this joy and peace that brings many people to the temple searching for answers and direction about specific challenges, problems, and situations in their lives.

Even when my children were very young, I tried to teach them to recognize personal revelation from the Holy Ghost, especially this feeling of peace. I remember once they asked if they could feel the Spirit.

"Absolutely!" I replied, and then did some serious thinking about what I could do to give them this opportunity. Finally I decided to take them to the Logan Temple.

We drove to Logan on a beautiful day. When we were there, we parked and I said, "Today would you like to feel the Spirit of our Father in Heaven?"

They answered with an enthusiastic, "Yes!"

"Okay, this is what we are going to do. First we are going to have a prayer and ask our Father in Heaven to let you feel His Spirit. Then we are not going to say anything to anyone, but we will get out of the car and walk each by himself around the Logan Temple. We aren't in a hurry; we can take our time. And we won't talk to each other."

We did this. The prayer was a simple one: we simply acknowledged the desire of the children to feel the Spirit and asked for that blessing. The children did as I had asked. As I walked ever so close to that sacred building, I could feel the Spirit. When we got back to the car, Dale, my oldest boy said, "Oh, Mom, is that what it feels like?"

I've had similarly strong feelings of peace at significant Church history sites, especially the Sacred Grove. If you walk into that sacred area with any degree of reverence, you will have an overpowering feeling of peace, which to me is a sure confirmation from the Lord that this is indeed a sacred spot. When I stand under those majestic trees and ponder the history of our Church and express gratitude for the Savior and the restoration, I feel little chills that run through all of me or part of me. Sometimes tears come. These feelings of peace are personal revelation sent from a loving Heavenly Father to reaffirm to me the truthfulness of the gospel of Jesus Christ.

One summer I was serving as a guide at the Visitors' Center at the Hill Cumorah Pageant. Everyone else had gone to lunch one day, and I was at the door greeting whoever might come in. One woman entered and stood still, just looking around. She had a look of complete amazement on her face, and

I almost hated to intrude. Finally I approached her and said, "Could I help you?"

"I cannot believe it," she said. "A number of years ago I visited the Visitors' Center at Temple Square in Utah, and while I was there I felt this neat feeling of peace. I have not felt it again until I entered this room today. What is it? It is wonderful!"

I had the opportunity of explaining to her that what she felt was peace given to her by the Holy Ghost, testifying to her that what was here was true. And of course the next question I asked was: "Would you like to have two representatives from our church come to your home and teach you about the Book of Mormon and answer your questions?" Her answer, of course, was yes.

Ultimately, of course, we don't need to travel to New York to feel the Lord's peace. And although we should attend the temple regularly, we don't even need to enter the house of the Lord to obtain the peace we seek. Peace is felt in our hearts and in our minds. This sacred feeling confirms truth, and truth exists almost everywhere in the world, whether we're driving down a traffic-logged freeway, hiking under a glorious, cloudless sky, or chatting with our children over grilled cheese sandwiches.

TRUSTING THE PEACE

As two elders in Bolivia returned home one night, they found a woman standing outside their door. She had a small bundle in her arms and her face showed her deep anguish. She explained that her two-year-old daughter needed a blessing. The child had been playing with some other children, who had placed her on the back of a large dog. She had lost her grip and fallen from the animal, and her head had struck a sharp rock. All night the child had run a high fever and cried with pain, but her mother could not afford to take the child to a doctor.

The young missionary who pronounced the blessing described how he pleaded in his heart with the Lord to grant him the right words and blessings to offer the child and her mother. But no words came to his mind.

Placing his hands on the child's head, the missionary began by stating the authority he held. His mind remained blank as he repeated a few familiar phrases. Later he said, "I have never prayed so hard as I did at that moment, silently pleading to know the will of the Lord concerning this tiny girl. Suddenly all my tension was replaced with a peaceful sensation, and the words seemed clear to me. I opened my mouth to speak, and in an authoritative voice I commanded the child to be relieved of her afflictions and to rest with no further pain. . . ."

The young elder closed the prayer and saw tears rolling down the faces of his companion and the mother. The child had stopped moaning. The missionary continued, "I assured the woman that everything would be fine. I felt certain that the Lord had helped me in bringing to pass His will concerning this baby. [She] covered her baby and then hugged me, thanking me for saving the child. I took the bundle from her arms, wanting to witness a miracle face to face. As I uncovered the baby's head and looked into her eyes, I realized she had died."

The mother nevertheless quietly thanked the two elders and left, leaving the missionary who had given the blessing confused and heartbroken. What had he done wrong? he wondered. Had he abused his authority? Then he felt the sweet message of peace. "For the second time that day, I felt the peace of the Holy Ghost as he testified to me that I had been an instrument in the Lord's hands and had said only that which I was prompted to say" (Bradley J. Dickerson, "Blessed with Peace," *Ensign*, February 1992, pp. 56-57).

Sometimes the feelings of peace we feel bring assurance from the Lord that all is right even when things don't end up the way we'd like them to. By exercising faith in the Lord and His perfect knowledge, we can focus on those feelings of peace and trust them, knowing that He is in charge and sees the big picture, and eternally all will be right in the world.

NOT THE WORLD'S PEACE

Much uncertainty invades this modern world. We read about wars and natural disasters in every newspaper. Young adults grow up fighting the temptations of drugs, alcohol, and immorality. Financial concerns bring terrible uncertainty as we budget for today's expenses, and tremendous fear as we think about college expenses, mortgages, and retirement. While long-term planning and frugal living are wise courses of action, there are no guarantees in this life. We could spend our entire mortal existence consumed with these terrible feelings and thoughts if we didn't have a promise of peace offered to us by Jesus Christ.

"Peace I leave you with you, my peace I give unto you: not as the world giveth, give I unto you. Let not your heart be troubled, neither let it be afraid" (John 14:27).

Even when common sense dictates that fear should exist in our lives, we can know differently as we seek feelings of peace from God. A fifteen-year-old young man described his feelings as his family was flying from Buenos Aires, Argentina, to Poadas, a town in the north Poadas. "I got a shiver down my back at the thought of crashing, but dismissed it. The plane was a little shaky, like me at that moment, but I was not terrified because I was with my family. . . . [Then] the plane started to tremble and shake a lot. That was when I felt terror. So I closed my eyes and, almost instinctively, said a prayer. . . ." As he prayed, he felt "a calm assurance that everything would be all right" (quoted by Vickie Groberg, "On a Wing and a Prayer," *New Era*, January, 1992, p. 9).

President Gordon B. Hinckley bore his testimony of the peace the Spirit brings in the words of the third verse of "My Redeemer Lives" (*Hymns*, no. 135), a hymn he wrote:

"Oh, give me thy sweet Spirit still,
The peace that comes alone from thee,
The faith to walk the lonely road
That leads to thine eternity."

Peace is crucial to have in our lives; living without the peace that comes from God means a life full of doubts, fears, hesitations, and uncertainty. Mortal existence promises each of us plenty of challenges, difficulties, and sorrows. We have a great need of our Heavenly Father's peace in order to maneuver our way through life's obstacles and return to a loving father and brother.

COMFORT

I had always heard about the "Comforter" in conference talks but never really understood what that was. I knew that the "Comforter" was the Holy Ghost but didn't comprehend how it could bring peace and comfort in a very special way.

However, the weekend I found out Sherm had terminal cancer was the beginning of my learning about the Comforter's role in our lives. At the time, Sherm and I had eight children; the youngest was a one-year-old baby, the oldest was fifteen. In between we had a fourteen-year-old, a twelve-year-old, a seven-year-old, a five-year-old, and three-year-old twins. I had terrible back problems and could hardly walk.

What a tremendous emotional, mental, and physical burden I felt! I wanted our home to be happy for the sake of our little ones, but I hurt so inside. I can remember more than once putting a meal on the table and getting the kids started, and then heading to the laundry room, where I would cry for a minute or two. Then I'd wipe away the tears and return to the table with a forced smile pasted on.

After about a week of this I went into my bedroom. "Heavenly Father," I began, "if you have to take him, you have to take him, but please will you take the knot out of the pit of my stomach so that I can be happy for the sake of the little children?"

We had the sweetest feeling of peace come into our home. One by one during the next three days, each of the three older children, who knew what was happening to their dad, came into the bedroom to talk to me. Although they had not talked to each other, they all had the same question: "Why, when things look so bad for us, do we feel that everything is so very right?"

I had the opportunity to explain to each one that what we felt was the Comforter. What we were going through might seem terribly difficult but in the eternal scheme of things we were right on schedule. The Comforter stayed with us some fourteen months until my husband passed away and then for about one month after that. What a great experience that was for all of us.

SUSTAINED BY THE COMFORTER

The Comforter, which is another name for the Holy Ghost, has a number of functions. According to John 14:26, it can "teach you all things, and bring all things to your remembrance." Other scriptures teach that it can also simply bring us a sweet feeling of peace and comfort (see John 14:27; D&C 6:23, 19:23, and 121:7).

"The Holy Ghost is also a comforter," said Elder Delbert L. Stapley. "It has the power to give peace to the soul of the righteous. . . . It is the Holy Ghost, or the Comforter, that fills us with hope and perfect love (Moroni 8:26). Men find peace, contentment, and comfort when by the Holy Ghost they gain a testimony of the Christ" (*Conference Report,* October 1966, pp. 113-14).

The Prophet Joseph Smith was sustained by the Comforter. This is obvious to us as we read about his trip to Carthage, Illinois, where he was killed. "I am going like a lamb to the slaughter, but I am calm as a summer's morning," he said. "I have a conscience void of offense toward God and toward all men" (Rulon T. Burton, *We Believe—Doctrines and Principles of The Church of Jesus Christ of Latter-day Saints* [SLC: Tabernacle Books, 1994], p. 631).

Sudden Thoughts, and Thoughts that Persist

7

"There came to my mind a thought. There was no voice, but just a thought."

—Thomas S. Monson

After a severe illness, a man became partially paralyzed. Whereas he had once been robust and healthy, active in many pursuits, he was now confined to his wheelchair. Despite the best of medical help and the fervent prayers of family and friends, Stan remained bedridden.

Elder Thomas S. Monson described how one day he suddenly thought of his friend Stan:

> I was swimming at the Deseret Gym, gazing at the ceiling while backstroking width after width. Silently, but ever so clearly, there came to my

mind the *thought:* "Here you swim almost effortlessly, while your friend Stan languishes in his hospital bed, unable to move." *I felt* the prompting: "Get to the hospital and give him a blessing."

Elder Monson quickly dressed and hurried to the hospital where Stan was staying. When Elder Monson found Stan's room empty, he asked a nurse where Stan might be found and was told that Stan was at the swimming pool, getting ready for his physical therapy. Elder Monson said,

> I hurried to the area, and there was Stan, all alone, at the edge of the deeper portion of the pool. We greeted one another and returned to his room, where a priesthood blessing was provided.

> Slowly but surely, strength and movement returned to Stan's legs. First he could stand on faltering feet. Then he learned once again to walk—step by step.

> Following his recovery, Stan frequently spoke in church meetings and told of the goodness of the Lord to him. Sometimes he revealed the dark thoughts of depression that engulfed him that afternoon as he sat in his wheelchair at the edge of the pool, sentenced, it seemed, to a life of despair—and how he pondered the alternative. It would be so easy to propel the hated wheelchair into the silent water of the deep pool. Life would then be over. But at that precise moment he saw me, his friend. That day Stan learned literally that we do not walk alone. I too learned a lesson that

day: Never postpone heeding a prompting. (*Inspiring Experiences That Build Faith from the Life and Ministry of Thomas S. Monson* [SLC: Deseret Book, 1994], pp. 47-48; emphasis added)

President Monson made it clear in this story that a specific *thought* came ever so clearly to his mind; he felt a prompting. He then knew what to do and acted quickly.

President Monson also describes another time when he acted on his thoughts. He was involved with a United Way campaign and had a meeting with the heads of the departments. At that meeting, some disabled children sang "I Am a Child of God."

"I was late for another meeting," President Monson recalled. "I walked toward the west door. *There came to my mind a thought.* There was no voice, but just a thought. It was, 'Forget the meeting. Shake the hand of each child.'"

He did so and testified of the joy he felt. "One child even kissed me," he said.

Afterward he felt 100 percent better. Later he discovered that the children had been told that if they prayed earnestly God would prompt President Monson to shake each one of their hands (told in a regional meeting in Salt Lake City, Utah, January 26, 1992; taken from the author's notes; emphasis added).

FROM TEXAS TO NEW YORK

When my second husband, Fred, and I went to get passport pictures taken, we were very impressed with Jeff, the man who helped us. As we talked and he found that I taught seminary, he said, "I don't usually share this story about myself but I feel I should."

Jeff, who was half Jewish and half Danish, received a mission call to serve in Texas. His stake president had told him that after he got his call he should pray about it and he would feel really, really good. He prayed about it and *felt terrible.* He told his stake president about his feelings and invited him to pray about it too. His stake president did and he also felt that there was a problem.

So the stake president wrote to President Spencer W. Kimball. In return, Jeff received a page-and-a-half, handwritten letter from the prophet! In it he received a new mission call to Rochester, New York. President Kimball also promised Jeff that he would be a good missionary and bring generations of his family into the Church. Although Jeff wondered how that promise would come to pass, he prayed about this new calling and felt right about it.

Soon after he arrived in New York, Jeff was transferred to Syracuse, New York, where he met someone who knew someone who had known his grandparents. This person introduced Jeff to some other Jewish people. Jeff enjoyed meeting them, but by the time his mission ended, he did not feel he had accomplished what President Kimball had told him he should.

Jeff sometimes wondered about that handwritten letter from the prophet, but didn't lose a lot of sleep over it. Then, years after he returned from his mission, Jeff received a box of genealogical information from one of the Jewish people he had met while on his mission. As he went through the box, Jeff found enough information to do thirty-five sealings for members of his family. He had, indeed, brought generations of family members into the Church.

But the story doesn't end there. When Jeff went to the temple to do the endowment work for his grandfather, as he approached the veil, he *thought* of a Jewish phrase. Jeff actually didn't know much Hebrew, and he had no idea what the words meant. But just before the veil ceremony, he uttered the words softly.

When he passed through the veil, the veil worker on the other side threw his arms around Jeff. With tears running down his cheeks, he explained that he was a Jewish convert. Just before he'd arrived at the veil, the same words—the same *thought*—had come to his mind.

The veil worker knew Hebrew and told Jeff the phrase meant "at long last—eternal life for me and my posterity." These were some of the same words President Kimball had used in his letter. It was almost as if the Lord had put the thought in Jeff's mind to trigger the experience at the veil and point out to him that President Kimball's prophecy about his family had finally been fulfilled.

"THE FEELING CAME OVER ME"

The Prophet Joseph Smith taught, "A person may profit by noticing the first intimation of the spirit of revelation; for instance, when you feel pure intelligence flowing into you, it may give you sudden strokes of ideas" (*Teachings of the Prophet Joseph Smith*, comp. by Joseph Fielding Smith [SLC: Deseret Book, 1976], p. 151).

In the December 1991 *Ensign*, President Gordon B. Hinckley shared a letter he had received. The man who wrote the letter described himself as a convert to the Church.

> Since age eleven I dreamed of finding the true religion, and fifteen years later I found it. . . . I have missed death as a child on more than one occasion, but a divine power has saved me every time.

> When I came to America [from Beirut], . . . I was given no hope in gaining acceptance into a medical school simply because I was not a United States citizen. A voice within me whispered that I would be a physician one day.

> I have attended one of the best schools in the country on a scholarship. I then went to another medical school for a reason totally unknown to me then. . . . A year later I was miraculously led to Church literature and joined the Church. Nine

months later I met my wife and we were married in the temple three months after we had met.

This man had a particular reason for writing to President Hinckley, as he explains below:

An hour ago I had a very special experience that led me to writing this letter. I was walking on my way home and a sudden feeling came over me that somewhere there is a young man who, except for money, qualifies to serve a mission for the Lord, and that I was to provide him with the necessary funds to serve a mission. I don't have any idea who and where this young man is, but the feeling came over me that you would know, and I was to put the funds into your hands and see to it that he serves his mission. That left me in tears. I arrived home and asked my wife how she felt after I had told her of the experience that I had just had. [She], of course, consented.

I am enclosing a check for $3,000 but the figure that came to my mind was $4,000. This is all the money that is available to us at present, but on January 27, we will send in another check for $1,000. I am still in my training as a physician. I have to work extra hours to earn a living for my wife and three daughters, and we do not have money for a down payment on a house. We have been trying for five years to save for a house, and the Lord has blessed us beyond measure.

Three years ago, a similar feeling came over me, but as we thought about it we felt that the Lord

was giving us a signal to be prepared to put at the
altar what he requires of us. We decided then that
once I am through with my training we will
support as many missionaries as our finances will
allow us. Tonight there was no doubt that the Lord
has asked us to put that money on the altar. . . .

We . . . leave the money in your hands to [use]
according to the inspiration of the Lord vested in
you. (*Ensign*, December 1991, p. 4)

This wonderful, humble brother had feelings he acted
upon. He also had a specific thought of the amount that was
needed. He knew the money was for a missionary, and he knew
he needed to send it to President Hinckley. Thoughts don't get a
lot more specific than that!

"MAKE THAT CAKE"

At times a thought may come to us suddenly and sharply,
so powerfully that a clear message is sent. Other times, the
message is more like a steady refrain that repeats itself over and
over, and will not subside until we act upon it. This persistent
thought is called a *recurring* thought because it *re-occurs*. It is
another way that the Spirit communicates with us.

On the day of the big BYU-U of U basketball game, Elaine
Beardshall wanted to make a blue-and-white cake (BYU's school
colors) and take it over to her neighbor, a loyal fan of the
University of Utah. But the day became hectic and Elaine found
she didn't have the time. When she mentioned it to her mother,
her mother replied that a call would do just as well; trying to do
too much always created too much stress. The thought kept
coming to her that she ought to do something more than call.

"I recognized that feeling," Elaine said. "I had experienced
it many times. But still I questioned: Why would the Holy
Ghost care if BYU won? Why did he so badly want me to

acknowledge that fact with [my neighbor] today? Couldn't the cake wait for a time that was more convenient for me?"

Later that evening, Elaine left a blue-and-white cake on the doorstep, rang the doorbell, and ran back to her house. Barely five minutes later, her neighbor was on the telephone calling to thank Elaine for "the most darling birthday cake [she had] ever had!"

That one act of service, concluded Elaine, caused their friendship to blossom, and their lives were greatly enriched and strengthened by their association ("Listen," in Michele Garvin, ed., *By Small and Simple Things* [American Fork, UT: Covenant Communications, 1996], pp. 37-38).

A Book of Mormon

Our daughter Merri was an obedient, hard-working sister missionary. One day a letter was read to all the missionaries in her mission in New Mexico. They were instructed to stop handing out copies of the Book of Mormon indiscriminately to children.

The next day Merri and her companion were on the street. Merri had a distinct thought come into her mind that she should give a Book of Mormon to a young boy who was standing there waiting for a bus. She reminded herself of the letter she had heard the day before, but she *knew* that boy needed a copy of the Book of Mormon. Again she reasoned herself out of it. When the thought came the third time, she thought, "Oh, what's one Book of Mormon?" She talked to the young boy for a minute and then gave him a book.

For the balance of the day Merri felt guilty. She knew what the letter had said: No copies of the Book of Mormon should be handed out to children.

That night as she and her companion returned to their apartment, the phone was ringing. When Merri answered it, a lady on the phone said, "We were on the bus today and on the seat of the bus was a Book of Mormon. We picked it up and have been reading it all evening. Your name and number were in the book. Could you teach us more about this wonderful book?" She and her daughter were baptized.

When promptings or knowledge comes, too often we let our mortal reasoning win out and we refuse to act on the feelings that come from our Heavenly Father. As we follow promptings we receive from the Holy Ghost, we discover that God knows what He is doing in our lives. These small successes give us courage and strengthen our faith so we can act on personal revelation received on larger matters. I have found that as I act on these promptings, I am less afraid to do so because my faith has increased.

"Move Your Car"

While my daughter Bonnie was a student at BYU, she borrowed her brother Dan's car to do some things that she needed to do. She got home late and temporarily parked the car in a tow-away zone. She was so very tired. The couch looked so inviting. She would just lay down for a minute.

She woke up in the middle of the night and the thought came to her, "Move that car out of the tow-away zone," and then she promptly fell back to sleep. A second time she awoke and had the same thought, followed by the same result. The third time that she woke up and the thought came, she looked and saw the car was still there. Only twenty minutes remained before she had to leave anyway, so once again she went back to sleep. This time it was a conscious choice.

When she woke up again twenty minutes later, she knew she had to leave. As she dashed out of her apartment, there was no car. It had been towed away. Three times the Lord had tried to spare this student from having to pay a $60 tow-away fee, and three times she ignored the prompting. God knew she lacked the money and had tried to help her.

I had an experience where I listened to a prompting and was very glad I did. One Saturday night I had a free hour before Fred and I had plans to go out for the evening. I had decided to work on my Sunday School lesson for the next day, but the thought kept coming to me that I should go see a young man in my class who was consistently absent.

At first I resisted. I didn't have a lot of time, and I really needed the time to prepare. Finally I decided to pay attention. So I called his home to see if he was there. Of course he was.

I gathered up some material from a lesson he'd missed previously and grudgingly went over. The young man wasn't feeling well and was in a terrible mood. We talked a bit, and by the end he had really softened up.

When I came home Fred greeted me in the entrance way. He knew I hadn't really wanted to make that visit. "How did it go?" he asked.

"It went soooo well," I said enthusiastically. "I felt the Spirit, and I think he did. It went soooo well," I kept repeating.

The next day that young man attended class, and he brought the Spirit with him.

When we listen to the *thoughts* that come to our mind, we will be blessed with spiritual experiences and the presence of the Holy Ghost. And I believe we are blessed with more and more thoughts that cover a broad range of subjects. We need to be sensitive to the promptings of the Spirit, even when they concern issues that we feel would not ordinarily fall under the territory of "spiritual."

"Ask for Their Dog"

Our nonmember neighbors in Burley, Idaho, had a black cocker spaniel dog, which my children adored. He was a very old dog, and he liked to come lay on our lawn in the shade. My children were very young, and they loved to pet him. All he would do was thump his tail a bit in response, much to the delight of the children. As a result of this sweet association they learned to love dogs.

One day I learned that these neighbors were going to move. The thought came into my mind, "You ought to ask if you can keep their dog."

"That's crazy," I told myself. "You just don't go up to your neighbors and ask for their dog!"

The thought persisted, so my husband and I talked about it. But it seemed out of the question. You just don't ask for someone's dog.

After our neighbors moved, I saw them downtown one day. I was very careful to say first of all, "We really do miss you." But then I went on and said, "You know, my children really miss your dog. Would you mind if we stopped by your new place and let them pet him?"

"Oh, our dog was such an old dog and we felt he would have such a hard time adjusting to a new place that we had him put to sleep when we moved" was their reply.

I was sick at heart over the prompting I had missed. But I had learned my lesson. I have tried especially hard since then to listen to the thoughts that come into my mind.

As we read Church publications or listen to the experiences of other Church members, it is interesting to notice how often people say that "a thought entered my mind." Sometimes when we are praying and mulling over a choice, all of a sudden a third alternative enters our mind. When this happens we explain to others that "I had this neat idea this afternoon." To be more precise, we might say that "God gave me such a neat idea this afternoon." And we must always remember to express thanks to the source.

BAD THOUGHTS

Just as God can put good thoughts into our minds—ideas that help us, motivate us, encourage us, or push us—we need to realize that Satan can and does put ugly thoughts there also—thoughts that tempt us, debase us, depress us, and encourage us to begin thinking all manner of evil.

We see this illustrated in Doctrine and Covenants 10:10 when Jesus Christ says in this revelation to Joseph Smith concerning the loss of the 116 pages of manuscript by Martin

Harris: "Satan hath put it into their hearts to alter the words which you have caused to be written, or which you have translated, which have gone out of your hands."

Notice that God says those ideas come from Satan. He repeats this idea in verses 13, 15, and 20. We also read in Moroni 7:17 that whatever persuades us to do evil comes from Satan. Numerous prophets of God have reminded us again and again that the "thought" precedes the deed. Our agency is what we do with those thoughts.

Through the Holy Ghost, God can plant all kinds of ideas that help us and help others. Recognizing that they come from Him encourages us to act on them. The more we act on them, the more we seem to receive. Recognizing that bad thoughts so often come from Satan can help us get rid of them. So often I will ask God to please help me remove the negative thought that comes to me. I also encourage my students to ask God to remove a bad thought when it first enters their minds. I know if we ask, He will do so.

URGENCY

8

"We have got to move and prepare for something big. . . .
We have got to put it on a red alert basis."

—Boyd K. Packer

When we returned from Brazil where my husband Sherm
had served as mission president, we felt an urgency to do three
things: pay off the house, obtain health and life insurance, and
accumulate our food storage. It surprised us that we felt this
way and we wondered about it; neverthless we acted on these
feelings.

We talked about these three things often during the next
two years, joking about how the neighbors could collect a can at
a time, but the Hibbert family had to hurry to get their food
storage together. I felt wonderful feelings of joy as I purchased
those green food storage cans. I was amazed that I could feel so
wonderful about that kind of a purchase.

Finally, in August of 1977, we went on one of our weekly dates. As we talked that night, we realized the feeling of urgency had left us. We had a decent food supply in our basement, our home was paid off, and we had our insurance. "We're finally ready for what the Lord has in store," we observed.

Within thirty days my husband was diagnosed with terminal cancer. Though it was a terribly difficult and tragic time, we felt deep gratitude for the urgency that had driven us to prepare.

GOD-GIVEN FEELINGS

One feeling that the Lord uses to communicate with us is a feeling of urgency. He might do this by giving us persistent, or recurring, thoughts. Sometimes an uncomfortable feeling accompanies the thought. The bottom line is that we feel a need to *do* something.

Elder Boyd K. Packer wrote of urgent feelings in his biography as he described the floods of 1983 in Salt Lake Valley. In the fall of 1982 winter came early. The Packer family lived along Little Cottonwood Creek, and they were concerned. "I sensed that we were in for something unusual," Elder Packer recalled.

At the time he was supervising the Utah Area with Carlos E. Asay of the Seventy. "I kept indicating that we should do something and suggested that Brother Asay not only contact the county but also get the Church organized to meet the possible emergency. He began in a casual way to organize. Along about February, they were still taking it up in this or that meeting. . . ."

Nevertheless, Elder Packer had "*deep feelings of impending trouble* and finally told his assistant and those working with him: 'Now you brethren are not listening. We are in for a terrible circumstance unless we prepare. We have got to move and prepare for something big. We must get all of the stakes along the Wasatch Front prepared to react immediately when this happens, because it is going to happen as certainly as we are sitting here. You emergency planners are taking a casual approach to it and we have got to put it on a red alert basis'" (Lucile C. Tate, *Boyd K. Packer: A Watchman on the Tower* [SLC: Bookcraft, 1995], pp. 281-82; emphasis added).

We can certainly sense Elder Packer's feelings of urgency. These were God-given feelings meant to guide him, and he obviously responded to them.

At least partially as a result of Elder Packer's urgency, sand-bagging was done along State Street, some flooding was averted, and much water was controlled.

"Run into the Orchard!"

Elder Bruce R. McConkie relates an experience where a feeling of urgency coupled with a strong thought and an immediate response saved his life.

As a boy, Elder McConkie loved riding horses. On this particular day he rode along a fence at the edge of the apple orchard. Suddenly something frightened the horse. It jumped and started bolting through the apple orchard. As it ran under some low branches, young Bruce was knocked out of the saddle. His leg got caught in the stirrup, but he was able to grab a saddle strap so his head did not hit the ground. It was difficult and tiring for him to hang on, but his life was at stake.

Elder McConkie's father was reading a newspaper in the house when the Holy Ghost urgently whispered, "Run out into the orchard!" Almost immediately Elder McConkie's father saw the horse, but he couldn't see Bruce hanging from the saddle on the other side. Nevertheless, he felt an urgency to stop the animal. It wasn't until after he'd obeyed that urgent prompting that he discovered his young son. Of course, he was most grateful that he had done what the Holy Ghost told him to do (*Teaching the Topics and Themes, A Beginner Course Teaching Manual* [SLC: The Church of Jesus Christ of Latter-day Saints, 1987], p. 91).

Urgent feelings can certainly change lives. One mother called me, very concerned about her daughter, Suzanne, who was living away from home. Suzanne had quit attending her church meetings and was very depressed. Knowing how much I loved her daughter, Suzanne's mother asked me to please write her a letter. "Maybe she'll listen to you," she pleaded. Of course I was glad to do it.

I thought about writing the letter from time to time. I even sat down to write it once, but as I sat at the computer nothing came to me. Eventually three weeks had passed, and I hadn't written a word to Suzanne. The next time I saw her mother I was embarrassed and apologized for not writing.

One Saturday morning some period of time later, I woke up about 6 a.m. and had a strong feeling that I needed to get up right then and write that letter. Now I am a late-night person and I had stayed up very late the night before. I didn't want to get up at 6 a.m. I thought about all the things I had to do that day. We had some nonmember relatives coming to stay for a while and I hadn't gone grocery shopping or cleaned the house; my Sunday School class group date was that evening, which also involved grocery shopping, as well as late-night adult supervision; and I had a Sunday School lesson to prepare. I knew I needed my sleep in order to handle all this.

But I could not go back to sleep. Thoughts of what I should write went through my mind. I felt the urgency to do it right then, and I was wide awake. I went to the computer, and the words just flowed. When I finished, I knew I had had help. The words of D&C 100:5-6 came to my mind: "Speak the thoughts that I shall put into your hearts, and you shall not be confounded before men; For it shall be given you in the very hour, yea in the very moment, what ye shall say."

I read the letter and knew I hadn't been the author of that one. I didn't make one single change. I simply printed it and gave it to Suzanne's mother.

"You know," she said, "I'm glad you wrote the letter now instead of three or four weeks ago. Because of a death in the family I think it will be better received now."

I don't know whether that letter made a difference in Suzanne's life. I only know God wanted it written and He wanted it written then. It is so joyful to be a part of something that God wants.

I do not know if some of you will distinguish between a "prompting" and the feeling of "urgency." To me there is a difference because the urgency leaves me no time to do something at a later time. For me it is more pressing than just a prompting. It is usually coupled with recurring thoughts, when a prompting occurs again and again, and I can't shake the feeling. This feeling of urgency is another way the Holy Ghost prompts us.

HOLIDAY URGING

One Christmas I found myself driving through town with more than enough to do when I felt an urgency to sign up as a substitute seminary teacher.

Now my husband and I have twenty-four children, including eight from my first marriage and thirteen from my second husband's first marriage. In addition, there are others who have lived in our home for extended periods of time that we consider our own. While not all of them were living in our home at that time, many were and we kept in frequent contact with the ones that weren't. The last thing I needed as I prepared for Christmas was to tack a seminary class onto the mile-long list of errands I already had to do around the holidays. But a feeling of urgency persisted. I learned long ago that God communicates in this way, and He knows best—but this was so very inconvenient.

So I found myself trying to argue with the Lord. "It's Christmas," I said. "I have plenty to do. I don't have time to sub now." It simply didn't make sense, and I had no idea how I'd cram that into my schedule. But finally, acknowledging the urgency, I gave in. "Okay, okay. Tomorrow I'll dress up and go apply."

The next day I went to Woods Cross High and met with the seminary principal, who sent me to an office in Farmington,

Utah. On the way, I stopped in and chatted with the seminary principal at Bountiful High and told him of my plans.

When I arrived in Farmington I was delighted to find that they couldn't get my name on the list of substitute teachers until the first of the year. It occurred to me that God had known this all along, but He also knew that to have my name on the list, I had to come in *now.*

I began substituting in January and in the spring was offered an opportunity to teach early morning seminary on a regular basis. I turned to the Lord for guidance; I was concerned with my family responsibilities, as well as obligations regarding my apartments. My logic told me I didn't have the time.

One evening a week or so later, as I stood listening to my son perform with an all-male high school singing group, I found myself asking the Lord: "Do you want me to teach seminary next year?"

Almost immediately I felt those tingly sensations that tell me I have an affirmative answer. I knew if God thought I could do it, then I could indeed do it. Since I began teaching, it has been a great source of joy in my life, and I stand in awe of the Lord's timing. I am so grateful for the urgent nudging that first got me involved.

MOVE TO UTAH

One evening after I gave a talk, a young sister came up to me. She was expecting a baby very soon, and she had two other children although they were not with her that evening. Tears poured down her cheeks as she shared her story.

She and her husband had been living in California. They were buying a home that they liked very much. He had a job that promised a bright future. They loved their ward and neighborhood. Life could get no better.

One day, out of nowhere, they felt an urgency to move to Utah. They didn't want to move to Utah; they were happy where they were. The feeling persisted for some time. They debated it, logically considering every aspect of a potential move. It just made no sense. They tried to shrug the feeling aside, but it persisted.

Finally, understanding the Lord as they did, they decided to move to Utah. They sold their home, he quit his job, and they came. While he hunted for work, their little family moved in with her parents.

He hunted and hunted for a job but found nothing. They questioned why they had done this as he continued his hunt. At the time it made no logical sense.

Finally in sheer desperation he had joined the army so at least he would have work. He was sent out of the state for his basic training, and she stayed with her parents since basic training was only a few weeks, and then they'd be transferred to wherever he would be stationed.

About three weeks into basic training he found out he had an incurable, cancerous brain tumor. "God does know what He is doing," this young sister said as tears rolled down her cheeks. "We had no health insurance when we were in California. With the army he has wonderful coverage. Also, I am already situated with my folks where the children and I get such strong support and love as we go through this terrible thing."

"TWO BOYS CLOSE IN AGE"

In the book she co-edited with her husband, *Each One a Miracle,* DeAnna Ball tells many inspiring stories of the miracles that were encountered in the adoptions of Romanian children by Americans. She herself experienced a miracle in the adoption of their two small boys.

After the birth of her fourth child, DeAnna felt strongly that she would have two more sons, close in age. Because of her difficulty in conceiving and carrying a child to term, she considered adoption. When Elder Thomas S. Monson told of the plight of the Romanian orphans in the April 1990 general conference, she had an instant reaction. "I knew," she said, "that one of those orphans was mine and I became preoccupied with the thought of adopting a Romanian orphan." Her husband, who was pursuing his doctorate and supporting the family on a part-time salary, asked her to wait until he graduated.

> I didn't talk about adopting in Romania anymore, but I could not get the idea out of my mind. One day the feelings were especially strong, and I poured out my heart in prayer to God, asking what I should do. My answer came quickly and directly. I did not hear any words with my ears, but the confirmation came straight to my soul—I would adopt in Romania. Strangely, though, I was instructed not to bother Terry about it. God would prepare the way for me, and I should wait and watch for that day.

Several months later DeAnna's husband came home, filled with the news that some good friends of his were going to Romania to adopt a baby. DeAnna said, "The same sense of urgency filled my being that I had felt nine months before. 'Oh,' I exclaimed, 'maybe we should go with them!'"

Her husband responded, "Wouldn't that be great?" That night he dreamed of cribs holding two babies and the next morning, he told DeAnna he wanted to adopt two children.

As Terry and DeAnna began to make their plans, DeAnna awoke one morning early in April with "an overwhelming impression" to telephone some people who had adopted Romanian infants. One of them warned her all adoptions would be suspended on May 1 and that unless they left immediately, they would not be able to adopt.

Terry and DeAnna made plans to go with another couple in their neighborhood, but DeAnna's husband could not get away from school and her neighbor's husband couldn't leave work. When DeAnna realized that she would be going without her husband, she understood that was the reason she had been prompted so many months before. "I began to understand why Heavenly Father had let me know a year in advance that I would be adopting in Romania. If I hadn't known for sure it was the right thing to do, I would have been too frightened to go." Many times while in Romania, DeAnna was guided by the Spirit and was at last able to bring home two small boys, close in age (DeAnna and Terry Ball, eds., *Each One a Miracle: Inspirational Romanian Adoption Stories* [Orem, UT: Grandin Book, 1994], pp. 152-53).

A FORCEFUL FEELING

A young mother related how the Spirit communicated with her to help her protect her daughter. "I was busily working in my kitchen," she said. "I suddenly had the forceful feeling that I should check on my tiny daughter. I didn't hear words, but I had an overwhelming *knowingness* that it was important to check on my crawling infant. She was sitting by one of the closets sucking on something."

Putting her finger into the child's mouth, she pulled out a small nail. Since it was a size the child could have easily swallowed, it could have done serious damage to her internal organs.

This mother also shared a second experience when the Spirit warned her that her daughter was in danger. As she was on her way to the temple, she had "an overwhelming feeling" that she should return home. She was almost to the temple and nearly dismissed the feeling. But it came again so strongly that at last she turned the car around and headed back home.

"It was dusk—just dark enough that cars have a difficult time seeing things outside clearly," she said. "As I turned my car onto the busy street where we lived, I saw my three-year-old daughter out in the street. I stopped my car, hopped out, and gathered her up in my arms" (Diane Bills, *Trust in the Lord* [American Fork, UT: Covenant Communications: 1996], p. 42-43).

PROMPTINGS

9

"The Spirit of God will reveal to [us] even in the simplest
of matters, what [we] should do by making suggestions
to [us]. We should try to learn the nature of this spirit,
that we may understand its suggestions. . . ."

—*Lorenzo Snow*

While my husband Sherm was serving as mission president, he felt driven to find people searching for the truth. He
envisioned a temple there in Brazil before anyone even dared
talk about it.

As the mission leaders, we organized motivational
programs for our missionaries every month. We sent copies of
the Book of Mormon on missions and we created "I Care"
programs. Well, Sherm felt prompted to launch a "Prepare for a
Temple" project.

"But Sherm," I protested, when he presented the idea to
me. "We can't promise these people a temple."

Sherm reminded me of a quote from one of the General Authorities that said, in essence, that the Lord would put temples wherever the people were ready. "We just need to help them get ready," he said, smiling.

Although my conservative nature was concerned that we were overstepping our bounds, I couldn't argue with Sherm's feelings, so we organized a temple project. We assigned leadership talks to the people who would introduce the program. We had missionaries cut and paste and draw large charts of temples to be posted in each of the meetinghouses. We created gold bricks to put on the temples representing each new baptism. We outlined ideas for sacrament meeting talks in our districts so that members were aware of what we were working on.

In the wee hours of that Sunday morning before the temple project was scheduled to be initiated, Sherm and I walked through the conference room where all the materials and charts were finally ready. I don't remember who said it first, but we both vocalized that something was wrong. We tried to decide what it was. Maybe the temple charts weren't big enough. Maybe a talk hadn't been assigned. We really had no idea. What we did know was that this was not to be presented the next day.

Sherm woke up the mission staff. It took all night but we prepared a different conference for that morning's meeting. For the next two weeks we continued to work on the temple project, significantly increasing the size of the temple charts and adjusting other materials.

Just a week after we'd finished refining the charts and materials, several Church leaders from Salt Lake City visited our mission while in the area for stake conferences. They asked that all members be invited to the Saturday night leadership meeting, instead of only those eighteen and older. That's all we knew about the meeting, although there was certainly a great deal of interest in what these leaders would say.

That evening faithful members gathered to hear inspired Church leaders. We sat in awe of how the Lord works as the theme of the conference was announced: Prepare for a Temple. There we were with talks, presentations, handouts, large temple charts, and gold bricks already prepared that would support this wonderful and inspired program.

The Lord prompted Sherm to prepare materials that needed to be available. However, our timing wasn't the Lord's timing, and he gave us uncomfortable feelings to stop us from distributing the materials too early.

STOP WHEN THE SPIRIT SAYS STOP

My youngest son, Dave, and I were proselyting in the audience at the Hill Cumorah Pageant. Time had passed quickly and it was time for us to be in our place on the hill for the beginning of the performance. We were quite late, and we needed to hurry. I had hip problems and was walking with the help of a cane. It would be difficult for me to make it to my place on the hill, and I had to allow more time because I walked so slowly. However, as we passed a young couple sitting on a blanket on the ground, Dave stopped me. "Mom, we need to stop and talk to that couple."

"We don't have time, Dave," was my quick reply.

"But Mom, we need to stop. We *need* to stop."

Knowing we didn't have time, I stopped and rattled through the dialog. I didn't do it with any feeling. I just rattled through it quickly. After all, we needed to be on the hill.

"We're Catholic," they said, and then there was a short pause. "But we would be really interested in filling out a referral card and having missionaries come to our home." They filled the card out quickly. The joy we felt at following a prompting was so great, we felt like we didn't need feet at all to get to our assigned spot high up on the hill.

"THERE WAS REVELATION THERE"

What is a prompting? Elder Gene R. Cook calls it a voice but then says, "As a rule, one must concentrate in order to hear the voice. It is generally *felt* more than it is heard" (*Receiving Answers to Prayers* [SLC: Deseret Book, 1996], p.71; emphasis added). Earlier I quoted Elder Richard G. Scott who referred to "the inner *feelings* that come as promptings from the Holy Ghost" (*Ensign*, November 1996, p. 75; emphasis added).

Promptings come in a huge array of feelings, thoughts, even instincts. "Sometimes we don't recognize them [personal revelations] when they come," said President Kimball. "We pray and pray and pray for wisdom and judgment and then we feel somewhat like we ought to go this particular direction. There was revelation there" (Edward L. Kimball, ed., *The Teachings of Spencer W. Kimball* [SLC: Bookcraft, 1982], p. 454).

Look at the chapter titles of this book to see what a variety of promptings there are. Too often we overlook the small, gentle promptings because we want the visions and visitations. "Expecting the spectacular, one may not be fully alerted to the constant flow of revealed communication," President Kimball reminded us (ibid, p. 457).

As you have been reading, it has probably become obvious to you that the term "prompting" can describe a variety of feelings, all of which come from God. Some General Authorities use the term "the Spirit." Others use the words "impressions," a "whispering of the Spirit," a thought that "came into my mind," an "uncomfortable feeling," an "urgency," a "knowledge" of something, a voice, the voice of the Spirit, a feeling of peace, or they might use other terms not listed here.

All of these serve as promptings. Heeding those promptings will bring all kinds of blessings into our lives. Sometimes those blessings will be recognizable, other times they won't. Sometimes promptings will make huge differences in our lives, other times we will be prompted to do things that seem insignificant, even worthless. But promptings to do good come from our Heavenly Father, and we must learn to recognize them and act upon them. As Moroni wrote long ago,

That which is of God inviteth and enticeth to do good continually; wherefore, every thing which inviteth and enticeth to do good, and to love God, and to serve him, is inspired of God. . . .

For behold, the Spirit of Christ is given to every man, that he may know good from evil; wherefore, I show unto you the way to judge; for every thing which inviteth to do good, and to persuade to believe in Christ, is sent forth by the power and gift of Christ; wherefore ye may know with a perfect knowledge it is of God. (Moroni 7:13, 16)

INVITINGS AND ENTICINGS

"The more we learn to pray throughout the day, the more the promptings will come and help us by inspiring us as to what to do," said Elder Gene R. Cook. "I have seen the gift of recognizing promptings manifest many times in my wife, who often has a feeling or impression about something that is needed or lacking in one of our children. When we follow these promptings they consistently lead us to additional experiences in faith" (*Receiving Answers to Our Prayers* [SLC: Deseret Book, 1996], pp. 71-72).

Psychologists say that we make seventy percent of our decisions based on how we feel about something. Obviously we want the Spirit of Christ in our lives, helping us feel right about good decisions. We must remember that the feelings that encourage us to do good come from God and those that encourage us to do evil come from Satan.

Personally, I don't differentiate between the feelings that come from the Spirit of Christ and feelings that come from the Holy Ghost. Trying to decide whether I'm feeling the Holy Ghost or the Spirit of Christ complicates the issue. Both sources lead us to God and come from Him.

Notice that Moroni says that that which is of God invites and entices us to do good. How is this done? The quiet urgings, the enticings, and the invitings come through feelings ever so subtle at times and at other times strong and urgent in their message. It is important to listen to these feelings and learn to discern which ones come from God.

Sometimes we'll receive a prompting that just doesn't make sense. I remember one evening I was preparing my Sunday School lesson and I had a feeling I should visit a young woman in my class. Her name was on the roll, but she'd never actually attended class.

It was about 10:20 p.m., a bit on the late side, and I still had a lesson to prepare. It didn't make sense to go visit a girl I didn't know at 10:20 at night. But I felt some degree of urgency, so I went. I just got in my car, drove to her house, and rang the bell. I greeted her with: "What do I have to do to get you to come to my Sunday School class?" I was surprised at my bluntness!

She talked about how hard it was to get up Sunday mornings. I agreed since I happen to be a late-night person, too.

"What do I have to do to get you to come?" I asked.

"I'll go in sweats tomorrow if you will," she said, with a sly look in her eye. "It will be easier than getting all dressed up."

"You've got a deal!"

"You're kidding? You won't really do it."

"I will," I said, "and I'll pick you up."

I didn't want my bishop to think he had a teacher with a problem so I telephoned him ahead of time to let him know what I was doing. He was delighted! And that young woman came.

I could have easily talked myself right out of that late-night visit, a visit that perhaps changed the course of direction in a young woman's life. But I knew the source of that prompting, and although I didn't exactly understand how one visit could entice or invite someone to do good, I knew from experience that following a prompting from the Lord is always right.

"Just One More Step"

Although we often receive promptings concerning ordinary, everyday activities in our lives, many people have told of promptings that have saved lives. While laboring in the Southern States as a missionary, President George Albert Smith had such an experience. He and his companion had been traveling all day, and it was late and very dark. Their destination was the McKelvin home, where they knew they would be offered food and shelter. The McKelvins lived on the other side of a high valley, and the two missionaries had to travel a high, narrow mountain path to get to their home:

> Our little walk was narrow; on one side was the wall of the mountain, on the other side, the deep, deep river. We had no light and there were no stars and no moon to guide us. . . .
>
> Our mode of travel of necessity was very halting. We walked almost with a shuffle, feeling each foot of ground as we advanced, with one hand extended toward the wall of the mountain. Elder Stout was ahead of me and as I walked along I felt the hard surface of the trail under my feet. In doing so I left the wall of the mountain which had acted as a guide and a steadying force. After I had taken a few steps away I *felt impressed* to stop immediately, that something was wrong. I called to Elder Stout and he answered me. The direction from which his voice came indicated I was on the wrong trail so I backed up until I reached the wall of the mountain and again proceeded forward.

Elder Smith followed his companion until they reached a fence piling, which they determined would be safe to climb over. When he was on top of the pile of logs, however, Elder Smith's suitcase accidentally came open and his belongings were scattered about. He retrieved what he could in the dark, but at the McKelvin home he realized that he had lost his comb and brush, so the following day they went back to the fence piling to look for them.

> I recovered my property and while [at the scene of the accident] my curiosity was stimulated and aroused to see what had happened the night before when I had lost my way in the dark. As missionaries, we wore hobnails in the bottom of our shoes to make them last longer, so I could easily follow our tracks in the soft dirt. I retraced my steps to the point where my tracks left the mountainside and discovered that in the darkness I had wandered to the edge of a deep precipice. Just one more step and I would have fallen over into the river and been drowned. I felt very ill when I realized how close I had come to death. I also was very grateful to my Heavenly Father for protecting me. I have always felt that if we are doing the Lord's work and ask Him for His help and protection, He will guide and take care of us." (Bryant S. Hinckley, *The Faith of Our Pioneer Fathers* [SLC: Deseret Book, 1956], pp. 90-91; emphasis added)

Certainly, falling off a precipice is a serious matter, and how grateful we are when the Lord intervenes in such large matters. However, we can be just as grateful that the Lord is concerned about small matters. One of my seminary students was gathering fast offerings one day. He came to a house on his "route" whose owners had never paid offerings. "These people never pay," he thought, so he put the slip and envelope between the slats of their fence by the gate.

About halfway down the street, the student stopped dead in his tracks. "Something told me to go back," he remembered. "The first time I didn't listen; I just started walking again. . . . This time I had a really strong feeling that made me turn around."

The young man returned to the house and knocked on the door. He was greeted by a blind woman who had her tithing check already filled out. She hadn't paid before because she couldn't see to fill out the slip.

Who knows? Perhaps that sweet sister had been praying for the chance to pay her tithing. This young man's obedience to a prompting brought blessings into her life, as well as his own.

A SURE GUIDE

As an early-morning seminary teacher, I have found that mornings can be hectic at my house. Some mornings I jump out of bed to answer the ringing phone, and the next thing I know I'm almost late for seminary. I'm off and running, and I've forgotten to say my prayers.

Finally I said to my Father in Heaven in a prayer, "Will you please prompt me to have my prayers in the morning just as I get up? I really don't want to forget them."

I want to bear my testimony that Heavenly Father will do just that. He will give you those gentle promptings. A thought will come to my mind just as I get up, reminding me to pray. God really meant it when He said, "Ask and ye shall receive" (D&C 4:7). He wants us to draw nearer to Him and He will help us do just that if we will let Him.

"The gift of the Holy Ghost is available as a sure guide, as the *voice of conscience,* and as a moral compass," said President James E. Faust. "This guiding compass is personal to each of us. It is unerring. It is unfailing. However, we must listen to it" (*Ensign*, April 1996, p. 4).

In *A Marvelous Work and a Wonder*, Elder LeGrand Richards, of the Quorum of the Twelve Apostles, stated, "It must . . . be understood that the Holy Ghost is the medium through whom God and his Son, Jesus Christ, communicate with men [and women] upon the earth" (SLC: Deseret Book, 1976, p. 119).

In order to start identifying promptings, you might want to write down a situation that you had a specific feeling about just to remind you of it. Doing this helps us identify what feelings and thoughts are our ideas and what feelings and thoughts are truly prompted by the Lord.

The Spirit urges us to do those things that are right. He puts thoughts in our minds, feelings of urgency, promptings and warnings. What great blessings these promptings are!

TINGLY SENSATIONS   10

"We do not have the words which perfectly describe the Spirit."— *Boyd K. Packer*

One year I was a volunteer in charge of a missionary preparation class at LDS Business College. We met in the ballroom on the top floor of one of the college buildings and invited youth from all over the valley. Each Sunday evening a returned missionary conducted the meeting, we sang "Called to Serve," and listened to a speaker. Sometimes I added a story or two. Then we divided into classes to learn about missionary work. Each class was taught by one or two returned missionaries.

After it was all over everyone gathered back in the hall for socializing and refreshments. Often these young returned missionaries who served so willingly as group leaders with this program helped more people get excited about missions around the refreshment table than in the classroom, although both experiences were wonderful for the youth who participated.

For activities, we sometimes did splits with the missionaries serving in the Salt Lake valley. Other times we just went proselyting with our own volunteer returned missionaries to get referrals for the full-time missionaries. The Spirit was always so very strong when I was involved with this program, and I went home each Sunday night full of the joy that the gospel brings.

Our attendance often numbered around 120 young people, with some youth coming from as far away as Kamas, more than an hour's drive away. Local seminaries used our program as makeup sessions for their seminary students. Strong seminary council members brought youth who were struggling because they knew that they would have an opportunity to feel the Spirit during the evening's activities.

However, as with all assignments from God, I felt a certain amount of conflict. It's never totally convenient to do the Lord's work. The program consumed a sizable amount of time to keep it organized. I spent every Sunday afternoon and evening with the missionary course, organizing it; during the week I was inviting speakers, looking for volunteer returned missionaries willing to help out, and preparing my own thoughts. I still had children at home, a weekly Sunday School teaching assignment in my own ward, and apartments to manage. By May I had decided to take the summer off. At the next missionary prep class, I announced that when summer arrived, we'd take a break.

I felt I'd made a very logical decision.

That night as the youth were returning to the ballroom for refreshments, the young man who came all the way from Kamas (some sixty miles away) said to me, "It has been so hard to come every Sunday night throughout the school year. It would be so nice to be able to come this summer when there's no conflict with my school schedule and homework."

Thinking about his words all the way home, I reminded myself of every logical reason why it was wise to let the class go for the summer.

I didn't even think about it on Monday. On Tuesday I was sitting in my room working on some papers when the thought crossed my mind, "You really should do that missionary preparation class this summer."

At the thought, tingly feelings raced through me. "You want me to have missionary prep this summer, Father?" I asked out loud. The feelings surged through me. But I asked again anyway, "You *really* want missionary prep this summer?" I could not deny what the Lord wanted, so the next Sunday I announced that I felt the Lord wanted the program to continue on through the summer.

I couldn't believe what happened next! As soon as school let out, our attendance shot up and we had 100 more youth coming to missionary prep. Our speakers for the summer were the best we'd had. The Spirit was so strong each time. Young people filled every chair and sat at the feet of the speaker, on the floor around the refreshment table, and on the window ledges. Sweat poured down our faces because it was hot and there was no air conditioning, yet those students returned week after week. As a result of our proselyting efforts, people were baptized and students committed to missions. The experience was a wonderful one for all of us involved. I am so grateful that God kept His program going for the summer. The joy I felt on a weekly basis was confirmation that those tingly sensations were from the Lord and we were doing right. That summer was one of the truly great experiences of my life.

Little Chills and Tingly Sensations

One feeling I watch for and can usually identify more easily than others I call *a tingly sensation*. Some people describe it as feeling little chills or shivers. Sometimes these little tingly sensations go up and down just part of me and sometimes it's as if I am plugged into them. Sometimes I feel them suddenly while other times they gradually move through my body until they fill me. Sometimes they are connected with deep, strong, warm, wonderful feelings and other times they are ever so slight.

Those of you who have these feelings know what I am talking about. Those of you who have not, watch for them. You may feel them anywhere, any time. Usually I can identify those tingly feelings with what I was thinking about or saying at the time I felt them, and when I feel them I know God is revealing to me that I just said or did the right thing or I'm on the right track. Sometimes He uses them to confirm the truth of what I was thinking at the time. Often I repeat those thoughts out loud to see how I feel.

In the May 1996 *Ensign,* Kirstin Boyer describes what she did that led her to have those tingly feelings. She said, "Every night, before I went to bed, I would read the scriptures. I would ponder and pray, asking my Father in Heaven if they were true. As I finished and climbed into bed, I felt a warm, tingly sensation through me. I knew my prayers were being answered."

Kirstin found that during the week she felt "happier and more helpful." School went better and she had enough time to study and do her homework. Her memory was more clear. She found time to continue her scripture study, and felt her testimony grow stronger. Even her relationships were better.

> Usually my mother and I argue about things, but that week I found the patience to listen and understand her point of view, which is something that isn't easy for me. I felt better about myself than I had in ages. . . . I felt worthier—all from reading the scriptures every night before going to bed. ("My Prayers Were Answered," *Ensign*, May 1996, p. 88)

The combination of scripture reading, prayer, and feeling the Spirit does make a difference in our lives. Feeling the Spirit so often comes after prayer and supplication to the Lord.

The Pageant Made the Difference

President Boyd K. Packer explains that "we do not have the words (even the scriptures do not have words) which *perfectly* describe the Spirit" (Lucile C. Tate, *Boyd K. Packer: A Watchman on the Tower* [SLC: Bookcraft, 1995], p. 279). I understand what he is saying, and yet here I am attempting to do just that, describe the Spirit. I have such a strong desire to help others become aware of how the Holy Ghost works because I have so appreciated His guidance in my life. I appreciate the assurance I receive that God will help me make right choices, guide me in the use of my time, and help me bear testimony of Him in a way that will influence the lives of the youth with whom I interact.

Not long ago I was reading my journal and I came upon this entry: "Brad opened his mission call tonight. He called me. I got to his home just minutes after he found he was going to the Panama Mission."

That short, succinct journal entry was actually the culmination of a very special experience where feelings, recurring thoughts, tingly sensations and a feeling of urgency combined to change the life of one young man I knew and loved.

Several years ago I was at church when the thought came to me that if Brad went to the Hill Cumorah Pageant, he would go on a mission. The feeling was so strong that when I saw Brad's mother a few minutes later I blurted it out.

"If we can just get that fine son of yours in the Hill Cumorah Pageant, he will go on a mission!" As I spoke, I felt tingly sensations, and I knew that the Spirit was bearing testimony that what I said was true.

"I'm getting those tingly feelings," I said. "Are you getting them, too?" She acknowledged that she was.

Now, at this time Brad was no longer living at home. Feeling a lot of conflict in his home situation, he had reacted by pulling away from the Church and moving out of his home while he went to college. At the time his mother and I talked, he was not even attending church meetings.

Brad's name kept coming to my mind so I finally got a pageant application and gave it to his mother. However, for various reasons she did not get it submitted until late in the fall and because it was so late, Brad was turned down. I called a man I knew who was associated with the pageant and pleaded for them to reconsider. I *knew* the Lord wanted Brad there. But due to the pageant's size and the number of people already accepted, no exception could be made.

The following summer the thought again came to my mind to get an application for Brad. I knew that somehow the pageant would provide the impetus and motivation for Brad to strengthen his testimony and gain a desire to go on a mission. I knew, too, that a testimony lay somewhere under all Brad's resistance to the gospel. The Lord would not let me rest until I obtained and delivered the application. I felt such an urgency to do so.

Unfortunately, once again the application was submitted too late in the fall to be accepted. Again I got on the phone and pleaded for his admission, but to no avail. Nevertheless, I couldn't deny the knowledge I had that if he would just go to the pageant, he would go on a mission.

The next July I again felt an urgency to get Brad an application for the pageant. This time I got the application early in the month, but Brad's mother said he wasn't interested in going. She and I talked about it and decided we would send the application in anyway, and we'd send it right away. I knew the earlier his application was mailed, the better his chances were of being accepted. If he got accepted, he could always turn it down; it wouldn't obligate him. But we knew God wanted him there.

In the spring his mom called. "I just learned that Bradley was accepted to the pageant," she said. "But now he can't decide whether or not he wants to go! He has to let them know by Saturday or he'll be dropped."

"Send him over to my house," I said. For two hours Bradley and I sat looking at my personal pageant pictures accumulated from four years of participation in the Hill Cumorah Pageant. I pointed out the fun he would have. As I told him many special pageant stories, we both felt the Spirit. When Bradley left, I asked him, "How sure are you that you'll accept the invitation to go to the pageant?"

"About 99 percent," he laughed. The next day he notified the pageant office of his acceptance.

We continued to talk about the pageant as Brad wondered if all the effort spent working out all the transportation details and costs would be worth it. But everything eventually began to fall into place. He found a ride to New York, and someone else gave him a ticket to fly home. I thought it was obvious that God had his hand in Brad's life as He made the way clear for Brad to be in this pageant.

When Brad returned, I expected a full report. But he didn't come to the house. I called him a few times, then got sidetracked with other matters. When I talked to his mother about three weeks later she told me that he had had a problem with some authority issues during the pageant, but that he had still found it to be a good experience. "Even though he'll never go on a mission, I'm definitely glad he went," she said.

I still believed that the pageant could be the means of getting Brad on a mission, so I called him and invited him to the missionary prep class I was conducting for the stake. "Bring your pageant pictures," I said. He came to the class and brought his pictures. Afterwards, we talked for a couple of hours. We talked about his questions, and I gave him the standard answers, standard because they're true: people aren't perfect and neither are leaders. Everyone is doing the best he or she knows how.

But I found myself pushing a mission too hard and had an uncomfortable feeling I had brought it up too often. We talked about the Spirit and the work, and when he left I said, "I think I have pushed a mission too hard, haven't I?"

He affirmed that my feelings were correct, so I apologized and told him I loved him, and he went on his way.

Imagine my surprise when only a few weeks later someone in the ward asked me if I'd heard that Brad was going on a mission! Brad came to my missionary prep class that night, and I just couldn't resist asking, "Well, have you decided to go?"

"Please don't tell anyone, but I did want you to know," he replied with a smile. I was soooo pleased! God knew all along what Brad needed, and then He let me and others know how to help. What a joyous experience that was!

IDENTIFYING THE SPIRIT

I often find myself saying to my seminary class, "Notice how we felt today in class. Do you feel that way in your English class across the street? What you feel here is the Spirit testifying to you that what we are talking about is true."

It is essential to identify these feelings from the Spirit, because if we don't recognize them, we can't act upon them. I encourage youth to heed any prompting, even if it's as simple as a *feeling* that they should stop and talk to someone in the halls of the school.

"Notice the feelings you have while you talk and as you finish the conversation and walk away," I counsel. "You might feel wonderfully happy or you might even have little tingly sensations. That's a confirmation from the Spirit that you did right."

Almost as important as recognizing these feelings and acting upon them is thanking God for them. I suggest to my students that as they walk away from the person they talked with to say to God in their minds, "Thank you for prompting me to stop and talk," and then notice how they feel. Sometimes tingly sensations and little shivers won't come until after we acknowledge our Heavenly Father's promptings and thank Him for them.

We can also identify the Spirit when we are sharing a spiritual experience with someone else and we feel that tingly sensation. That is, to me, a confirmation of the Spirit that what we said was true. As in my seminary class, I always like to identify those feelings and ask the other person what they are feeling.

Not always, but often, they reply, "I feel these little chills," or "I have this tingly sensation." But sometimes they can't find the words to describe what they are feeling. This provides the perfect opportunity for me to follow up with, "Do you realize what that is? It is the Holy Ghost verifying to you that what we were talking about is true."

Missionaries know these feelings. These feelings or some combination of wonderful feelings are what they feel as they tell the Joseph Smith story in their missionary discussions and as they testify of the truth. These same feelings should substantiate decisions they make following their missions when they have fasted and prayed for the Lord's help and guidance. Of course we are free to make all of our decisions on our own, or we can make them based on what God helps us feel is right.

MY BROTHER'S KEEPER

Obviously, if we make the choices the Lord wants us to—even when they are choices that don't seem to make sense to our logical self or choices that we simply don't want to make—we will be blessed. And often in the process we bless others.

Scott grew up in a terrible situation, moving around from home to home since he was twelve. When we met him and learned of his situation, we invited him to live with us for a few months as he prepared to go on a mission. We really grew to love Scott, and he responded well to living in our home. As the date neared for him to enter the MTC, we all felt great joy and anticipation.

One day as Scott and I were talking, he mentioned that his brother Jacob would soon be without a place to live. I was surprised at Scott's concern because although I knew he loved his brother, their association had been a terrible source of conflict, abuse, and contention for Scott.

Shortly after Scott told me about Jacob, I was doing the laundry. I often talk to Heavenly Father when I'm folding the laundry, and during this conversation I remember asking, "Would you want us to take Jacob into our home?" Those little *tingly* things went through all of me, and I felt the Spirit very powerfully.

I was startled at the response because I knew Scott had found security in the walls of our home, and my logic said that bringing his brother into our home might threaten that security. I loved Scott and didn't want to do anything to threaten those feelings. Besides, we hardly knew Jacob. I wasn't sure I wanted to get involved.

So I asked again, "Do you want me to take this young man into our home?" The Spirit answered very clearly. In utter disbelief I asked a third time, and the response was the same.

Still, I didn't act on my feelings for a week or two. My logical self kept saying that Scott had finally found a safe spot in our home, and it just wouldn't work if we tried to share that spot with his brother.

I didn't tell Scott about the feelings I'd had, although occasionally I would ask if his brother had found a place to live. "He's not even looking," Scott answered each time.

One day Scott and I went to the Salt Lake Temple together. We both loved spending time in the celestial room there. While I sat and enjoyed that special place, I had time to pray about every member of my family.

My thoughts then turned to Scott's brother Jacob, and I told Heavenly Father, "You know and I know how I feel about this situation. I have a major concern about maintaining Scott's security level, but if you want me to take Jacob, please let Scott suggest it. At least that way he can still feel safe in our home."

After the temple session we drove up to Capital Hill and found a beautiful spot to read Scott's patriarchal blessing.

Although there was much in it he did not understand, it was a wonderful blessing. We came home, talked a little more, and then Scott went to bed. I got a glass of orange juice out of the fridge and then headed to my bedroom.

There at the head of the stairs stood Scott.

"Mom," he said, which was what he called me. "Will you please take my brother, Jacob?" The Spirit spoke to me very strongly as tears ran down my face. How could I deny the will of the Lord?

Later Jacob told me how his testimony had been growing over the previous four months although at the time he was not even thinking of a mission. One day he was reading about Alma the Younger, and he found himself saying to God: "I don't know how, but is there some way I can serve you?"

When he learned that he could no longer stay with the family he had been living with, Jacob prayed again. He asked for a place to live that would be really good for him and where everything would work out where he could also have a good senior year in high school. He said, "I felt so calm. I knew I was going to be okay. I knew I didn't have to worry." So he did nothing to even attempt to find a place to live.

Jacob came into our home the day after Scott entered the MTC, and what a joy he became. He had a wonderful senior year, interacted with my own son in a special way, earned a scholarship, and went on a mission. Best of all, by sharing our home, Scott and Jacob share a remarkable relationship. As always, God knew exactly what He was doing in bringing both Scott and Jacob to our home.

"THIS ONE IS A RIGHT ONE"

I love to be used by the Lord in serving and helping others, and when I feel those tingly sensations, I know I can be used if I will act as I'm directed. One day the mother of a young woman I knew telephoned me. She was very worried about her daughter Claire. Claire had been in her late teens when this mother and

her husband had adopted her, and the abusive treatment Claire
had received before the adoption had left its mark on her life.
She just wasn't quite like other girls her age. This loving mother
expressed concern about whom Claire would date and what
would become of her.

Although I listened and sympathized, I didn't feel there
was much I could do to help.

A few weeks later I attended BYU Education Week. I
remember that several speakers mentioned that coincidence is just
the Lord working anonymously. I like to think this is what
happened, because within a week I received a phone call. The
caller, who lived in another city, wanted to know if I knew anyone
she could line up with a special young man. As soon as she asked
if I knew anyone, Claire's name came to my mind. As I gave this
caller this young woman's name, I felt those tingly sensations,
which I knew was the confirmation of the Holy Ghost.

"Do you know anyone else?" the caller asked.

"You don't need any other names. This one is a right one."

These two young people are now sealed in the temple for time
and all eternity. They have a beautiful baby and are very happy.

A Choir of Fifty

Good music often stimulates these tingly sensations,
especially if your heart and mind are focusing on the message
of the music. I love the story that Sister Patricia Brower related
in the *Ensign*. Sister Brower was a Primary president in a small
Nevada town. She wanted her Primary children to participate
in a service project so that they might experience the joy of
giving during the winter months so close to Christmas. So
they planned to visit a local senior citizens' center and present
a program.

One of the musical pieces they chose to perform was the
beautiful children's carol "When Joseph Went to Bethlehem."
The children loved the song although they had difficulty
learning both verses.

Shortly before the day of the activity the sister who led the singing found a job, which meant she might have to miss the performance. The Primary leaders seriously considered canceling the service project since so few people knew how to lead music, but they finally decided to keep the appointment at the senior citizens' center anyway.

On the appointed day, the children began to assemble at the church. "My heart sank, however, as I looked over the group gathered in the cultural hall and realized that only half of our Primary had come," Sister Brower recalled. The regular chorister hadn't shown up yet, so another sister agreed to substitute until she arrived—if she arrived.

Before heading to the center, the children ran through the program once. Although they did their best, the volume was weak, the words uncertain and hesitant. The worst song they sang was "When Joseph Went to Bethlehem." The children barely managed to stumble over the words. Said Sister Brower:

> After words of encouragement to the carolers and a fervent, heartfelt prayer for divine help, we filled the cars with children and drove to the senior citizens' center. To our amazement our regular leader was waiting there for us. The children took their places. I breathed another silent prayer and played the notes of the introduction to the first carol. I was astounded by the clarity and ringing quality. . . . As they went on the music increased in volume and the faces of the children radiated joy and confidence. I could hardly believe my own ears as they sang "When Joseph Went to Bethlehem." The words rang out, clear and strong. The teachers quietly wept, and *I felt chills run up and down my back* as the chorus of 25 sang like a choir of 50.

At the end of our program, we wished our new friends a merry Christmas and went out into the radiant December sun. I listened to the children speak in wondering tones to one another. One little girl said to her friend, "I didn't know the words to the song about Joseph, but I sang them anyway!"

Many years have passed since that December, but the memory is as vivid as though it were yesterday. In that tiny Nevada hall, our humble, struggling Primary was part of a miracle. We heard the herald angels sing. (Patricia Brower, "We Heard the Herald Angels Sing," *Ensign*, December 1991, p. 27; emphasis added. Used by permission.)

Sister Brower recognized that the Spirit was with these children through the chills that she felt and also through the children's increased capabilities. This confirmed to her that they had indeed received special assistance so they could perform their program well.

A No-Vote Date

Sometimes when I'm trying to make a decision or trying to figure something out, I say to my Father in Heaven, "The best thing for me to do in this situation is this: . . ." And then in my prayer I outline what I think is best and ask Him if my plan is right. Afterwards, I always pay special attention to how I feel. Sometimes, but not always, I will feel the little tingly sensations, and then I know my choice is a good one. Other times I don't feel very good about my choice until I'm further down the road, but when the feelings come, I know then my choice is a good one. Still other times I feel peace.

When I was teaching the seventeen-year-olds in Sunday School, I established the practice of saving all the lessons that had anything at all to do with dating and teaching them all together for several weeks in a row. The young people loved this group of lessons.

At the end of this series of lessons everyone wrote on a piece of paper the characteristics they wanted in a person they dated. Then that Sunday afternoon all the young men would come over to my house, read the papers the young women had written, and carefully choose a friend or classmate to go out with each young woman in the class, someone who best matched the characteristics the young woman had listed.

A little later the young women came over and did the same for the young men. Before the day was over, everyone in class had a date for our class activity.

The group date we planned was generally based around some type of service project, along with food and another fun activity. Usually I would make a few phone calls and visit a few places that might need our services, then I'd list several options in class and let the young people decide what they wanted to do.

One year I contacted a lady who was in charge of volunteer work at a local community hospital to see if they had any need for our help. As we spoke I felt the Spirit very strongly. In my mind I asked the Lord if it was right that we should come here for our service project. Then I paid special attention to how I felt. Once again I felt those tingly sensations running through my body.

"Normally I would let you vote on where you want to go," I told the class. "But I want you to know that the Lord wants you at South Davis Community Hospital, so this year I recommend that there be no vote."

The youth responded beautifully; I had their full support. We had almost fifty people the night we went to the hospital. We spread out over three floors and became involved in several different projects. We couldn't have had a finer experience. The Spirit was strong that night, and the youth acknowledged it. They felt the joy and happiness that come when you do what God wants done and when you serve. "But the fruit of the Spirit is love, joy, peace, long-suffering, gentleness, goodness, faith . . ." (Galatians 5:22).

GIVEN THE RIGHT WORDS   11

*"Speak the thoughts that I shall put into your hearts,
and you shall not be confounded before me; For it shall
be given you in the very hour, yea, the very moment
what ye shall say."—D&C 100:5-6*

Elder Carter was extremely negative. He couldn't find
anything positive to say about anything at all. Any suggestions
as to the day's activities were always treated with scorn.
Anything that went on in a district meeting was not right. He
put down anybody who said anything at all about anything. As
Elder Carter's mission president, Sherm transferred him every
thirty days because he felt that thirty days with him was enough
punishment for anyone.

One morning I was sitting at the mission home when one
of the mission home staff elders knocked on the door. "Oh,
Sister Hibbert, what should we do?" he asked. "Elder Carter got

so irritated and angry this morning that he picked up a knife and attacked his companion."

Sherm and his assistants were out on a round of mission conferences. I was expecting a baby at the time and wasn't able to travel. But I would have preferred traveling to dealing with Elder Carter.

After making sure that Elder Carter's companion was more frightened and angry than hurt, I told the mission office staff to put Elder Carter in my husband's office. "I'll be down in just a minute to talk to him," I said.

I got down on my knees and begged for help. I didn't know what to do. I knew that Elder Carter already knew that he'd done a wrong thing. For me to go say, "That was wrong," was rather useless. I didn't know what to say.

I pleaded with the Lord for help. I wished He would just write the answer in the carpet, and I would just go do whatever he told me to. But the Lord doesn't work that way. I remember reminding the Lord that I hadn't asked for this job, but that I would like to do it the way He wanted me to do it; I just didn't know what to do. I felt nothing at all.

Finally I got off my knees and went downstairs. I stood in front of the door of my husband's office pleading with the Lord for help. I still did not know what to say.

I entered the office and, because I did not know what to do, Elder Carter and I chatted. We chatted for an hour and fifteen minutes. We talked about everything he liked and everything his brothers and sisters liked and classes and anything else I could come up with. All the time I had a prayer in my heart.

All of sudden I knew what to say. I take no credit for what happened next. I just knew what to say. "Elder, are you enjoying your mission?" I asked.

"I think I would, but I have a slight problem," he replied.

"And what is it?"

"I think I have a tendency once in a while to be a little bit negative." *Now that's an understatement,* I said to myself.

"Well, I have the solution to your problem."

He was interested. "What is it?"

"Whenever anyone says anything to you, anything at all, I want you to always say two words. I don't care if you mean it or if it is true. I just want you to say it."

"What are they?"

"I won't tell you until you commit," I said, smiling. With some encouragement he finally committed to saying the two words, whatever they were.

"I want you to say, 'That's great!' Can you do that?"

Elder Carter agreed, and I had his companion come in. "What are you planning to do this afternoon?" I asked his companion. He was rather hesitant to make a suggestion. After all, the last time he'd made a suggestion, the knife came out. But finally he outlined a few possibilities.

"How do you feel about that?" I asked Elder Carter. He looked at me kind of funny and said, "That's great." His companion just about passed out.

"And then what do you plan to do after that?" I asked. Elder Carter's companion was a little quicker with his answer this time.

"And how do you feel about that, Elder Carter?" I asked again. "That's great!"

I heard it four times in the office and then as they walked down the hall I put an arm around Elder Carter and whispered, "I want to hear it two more times before you leave." I did.

The beautiful part of the story is that not that month but the next month those two elders were the top two baptizing elders in our mission, and we never again had a problem with Elder Carter. God knew the answer, but He allowed me to sweat it out to the last minute before He helped me, giving me the very words I needed to help this young missionary.

"The Very Moment"

In John 14:26 we read, "The Comforter, which is the Holy Ghost, . . . shall teach you all things, and bring all things to your remembrance, whatsoever I have said unto you." In D&C 100:5-6 the Lord promises us: "Speak the thoughts that I shall put into your hearts, and you shall not be confounded before men; For it shall be given you in the very hour, yea, the very moment, what ye shall say." Together these two scriptures make it clear that the Holy Ghost will put words in our minds for us to say.

An incident in the life of President Lorenzo Snow illustrates prophetic words that were given to him. He had become President of the Church in September 1898. With this responsibility he faced intense financial problems because the Church had indebtedness that amounted to about two million dollars, much of which bore ten percent interest. How was the Church to pay off this tremendous debt when the interest alone added up to more than most people of that day could imagine?

President Snow went in prayer to the Lord to learn what he should do. The strange and unexpected response was that he was to go to St. George, for a reason that was completely unknown to him. At that time southern Utah was experiencing a long, severe drought, possibly the most severe in its history. Several years with inadequate moisture had caused both streams and wells to completely dry up. According to the U. S. Weather Report, 1898 was the driest year ever recorded in the history of St. George. Thousands of cattle had been lost, and the frosts had damaged the grape harvest. The residents of the town were sadly disheartened. President Snow said: "All through Dixie, we found everything drying out. The stock were dying by the hundreds. We could see them as we were driving along. Many of them being nothing but skin and bones and many were lying down, never, I suppose, to get up again."

People were so discouraged that although it was nearly July, many refused to plow their land and plant seeds for another crop. Some had already left the area and others were planning to leave soon.

A conference was called in St. George. People came from far and near to hear the aged President, who was accompanied by many of the General Authorities of the Church. When he arrived there, President Snow did not know just why he had gone to St. George except that the Lord had directed him to do so. In speaking, he referred to the serious [drought] conditions and was inspired to promise the people if they would observe the law of tithing from then on, remain faithful, and be honest with the Lord, that they might go ahead, plow their lands and plant their seed. The power of heaven rested upon him and he promised them in the name of the Lord that the clouds of heaven would gather, the rains would descend, the lands would be drenched, the rivers and ditches filled and they would reap a bounteous harvest that very season. He further promised that the rains would continue if the Saints would remain faithful and the land would be fruitful.

This prophecy was made on the 17th of June. The people believed confidently that this declaration of the venerable President would be fulfilled. Not only did they pay their tithing, but they plowed their lands, planted their seed and proceeded with perfect assurance that all he had promised them would be fulfilled if they would do their part.

However, no rain appeared to be forthcoming. After President Snow returned to Salt Lake City, he paid careful and anxious attention to the weather reports. As the summer days passed, the crops continued to dry up. Skeptics began to question, and President Snow's soul was deeply burdened. His son LeRoi, who served as his father's private secretary, watched as the summer's events evolved toward a dramatic fulfillment of prophecy:

> It was the beginning of August and the heavens were still as brass over their heads. The crops were in dire need of moisture. LeRoi went to the Church office one morning and his father was not there. They told him he had gone to the Beehive House where he lived, and so LeRoi went over and as he ascended the stairs leading to his father's bedroom, he heard the President's voice and saw him, through the door which was ajar, kneeling before the Lord, and he reverently listened to him pleading with his Father in heaven for rain, explaining that the people had been obedient to His word; they had paid their tithing, plowed their land, planted their seeds and no rain had come to reward them. LeRoi said that he could never describe the fervor with which his father pleaded with the Lord in behalf of the people for rain—it must come soon or the crops would be lost. Almost immediately thereafter word came from the south that the clouds were gathering and it looked like rain, and soon thereafter word came that it was raining. The rain descended, their lands were drenched, the rivers and the ditches were filled, and they reaped a bounteous harvest that very season. . . . No sooner had it started to rain than the aged President retired again to his bedchamber and poured out the gratitude that filled his heart to overflowing because the Lord had heard and answered his appeal.

President Snow made his prophetic promise on June 17 and the first rain appeared on August 2. The crops and cattle were saved and the Saints were encouraged as they witnessed the literal fulfillment of a prophet's words.

The Saints throughout the Church were inspired to pay their tithing, which allowed the Church to pay its debts in only three years (Bryant S. Hinckley, *The Faith of Our Pioneer Fathers* [SLC: Deseret Book, 1956], pp. 50-53).

Note that words were given to President Snow to make promises, but they were given to him as he stood in front of the congregation in St. George. He didn't even know why he was going to St. George; he only knew that the Lord wanted him there.

So often the Lord will test us and leave us until the last minute before bringing forth His blessings. He certainly tried the people in St. George as well as President Snow. President Snow asked the Lord repeatedly for the fulfillment of that prophecy, acknowledging that obedience, effort, and faithfulness had taken place. It was only after much pleading that the Lord answered those prayers. D&C 4:7 reminds us to ask and *then* we will receive. We must remember that even a prophet has to ask repeatedly for blessings and guidance.

FILLING YOUR BUCKET

So even though we are not prophets, will the Lord give us the words that we should say in a particular situation? Yes! The same scriptures hold true for each of us. He works with seminary teachers, bishops, counselors, parents, and youth.

Some of the most powerful experiences I've had with the Lord giving me the very words I should say have occurred in the classroom. I first had this experience as a young married sister in a ward in Moscow, Idaho.

I had been called to teach the Spiritual Living class, and Sister Christensen, the Relief Society president in the student ward we lived in, explained that I had been called because she wanted the young sisters in the ward to feel the Spirit during the lesson, and she knew that I could teach lessons on that level.

I was overwhelmed with that responsibility and wondered how I could teach with the Spirit. I seriously questioned my ability to consistently teach with the Spirit.

Sherm, however, was a source of comfort and advice. He encouraged me to (1) study my material well and outline the lesson plan, (2) pray and ask the Lord for help, telling Him of the Relief Society president's expectations, and (3) go with a prayer in my heart and the flexibility to follow whatever thoughts entered my mind.

I did all of that. That first morning as I stood in front of the sisters, all of sudden I felt like beginning with Idea #2 on my outline. And then I used question #6, and as the lesson unfolded *it was right and I knew it.*

A story came to my mind that was not in the outline, and I used it. I knew that God was helping me. It *felt wonderful* and I knew the sisters were feeling the Spirit.

That was the beginning for me. I am so grateful to Sister Christensen and her expectations and to Sherm for outlining what I needed to do and to God who answers prayers.

Those same steps apply to teaching any lesson or presenting any presentation. For instance, if you're preparing a Sunday School lesson, first study your lesson and do your best to outline it, preparing it with the needs of your class in mind.

Next, pray and ask the Lord to give you the words at the very moment that are best for you to say. Ask Him to put thoughts and ideas in your mind that will reach the hearts of your class members.

Then enter your classroom with a prayerful attitude. I've heard someone say that the Lord works best with a full bucket. In other words from the reservoir of study that you have done come ideas in a better sequence than you prepared.

As teachers in the Church, we have a wonderful support system! Who better can you have in your corner than Heavenly Father and His son, Jesus Christ?

A SECOND CHANCE

When I was teaching a seminary class that started just after lunch, students had a tendency to come late, not early. One day, however, one of my students, Monte, came early. I listened to him talk and realized that no one in his family went to church. None of his family were members, except for his mother, who was actually investigating another church! Monte wasn't going to church and wasn't even planning on taking seminary anymore.

Before I could really respond to Monte, it was time for class to start. And when class was over everyone, including Monte, hustled out the door so they could get to their next class on time.

I didn't feel good about the conversation I had had with Monte. The semester was almost over, and it was late for me to learn about his background. I should have learned more about him earlier. I felt I hadn't said anything helpful to the young man. I chastised myself as I drove home that day and asked my Father in Heaven what I should have said. Into my mind came ideas so sure and strong that I stopped my car on the side of the road and wrote them down. I knew their source, and I did not want to forget them.

Now that I had the words Heavenly Father wanted Monte to hear, I needed a chance to talk to him again. I asked the Lord if He could bring Monte back to class twenty minutes early the next day. Even as I prayed, I knew that I was asking a lot. Monte's lunch break was only thirty minutes long. I needed twenty minutes of that time, but I know how precious food is to teenage boys.

Oh me of little faith! I really didn't really expect Monte to show up, but the next day, twenty minutes before class, in he came. I had the choice opportunity of pointing out to him that he is the one who will have the opportunity to teach his family the gospel. To do so, he needed more seminary, not less. And he needed to start attending his church meetings. As we talked about how he could do this, we both felt the Spirit very strongly as God confirmed the validity of that conversation. That day Monte committed to start attending church.

In this instance my bad feelings spurred me into action to find out what I should have said. And then, when I turned to Heavenly Father for help, He told me what I should say. The Spirit confirmed the truth of my words during our conversation so that both Monte and I felt the Spirit. And I think it's safe to say that Monte must have had some kind of feeling prompt him to skip lunch and come to class twenty minutes early, two days in a row.

This kind of help is available for every young person, every parent, and every leader. A parent can pray about a problem with a child, pleading for the Lord to help him communicate in a way that his child will understand.

"Help me, Father, to be perceptive to my child's needs, to really hear what she says and then give me the words to say what will help her most."

God knows a whole lot more about our children than we do. In a home where there is a wall built between a parent and a youth, both might plead with God to be given words that will soften hearts, break down walls, and hasten understanding. When we pray, asking for the very words we need to say in any given circumstance, we allow God to enter our lives and help us.

Often, by uttering these God-given words, we also help others. I remember receiving a phone call one day. A special person was having serious marital problems. As we talked, I prayed silently in my heart. All of a sudden *I knew what to say.* I felt the Spirit so strongly, and *the words just flowed.* The advice was right and I knew it. Afterwards I got busy doing other things and then I decided I wanted to write down what had been said because it was so wise. I could not and still cannot remember one word. But this I know: it was what God wanted said at the time. It was truly an example of Doctrine and Covenants 100 where the Lord said He would give the words at the very hour.

THE LETTER I COULDN'T WRITE

When I was just thirty years old, my husband was called as a mission president in São Paulo, Brazil, and I became a mission "mom." What a marvelous experience to have 200 young elders and sisters to watch over!

At one point we learned that a young elder who was serving in Campinas had contracted spinal meningitis. That scared us all because it could be fatal or leave severe permanent damage. The elder was very sick, and the instructions I had been given were to notify the family when an elder or sister was seriously ill. I sat down to write the letter and just could not do it. I didn't feel comfortable about it, so I put it off for a day.

The young man was in critical condition. He was having blessings daily, and we all prayed for him. Again I sat down to write the letter, but I couldn't. I went and visited the missionary at the hospital. I saw firsthand how ill he was. I told myself I had to write that letter, but no words would come. I felt uncomfortable about it, and so I just kept putting it off.

Finally the young man went through the critical part of his illness and I knew he was going to be okay. Only then did I sit down and tell the family what had happened, reassuring them, of course, that he was past the critical point and he was going to be totally fine.

Then for the next fifteen years every time I thought of that elder and that situation, I felt guilty because I did not write and tell his family when that elder was so very sick. Finally the young man came to a mission reunion. When I saw him, I said, "I've been on a guilt trip for years because I did not immediately write your folks and inform them of your very serious condition."

"I am so very grateful," he replied. "You see my dad is a medical doctor and he would have flown me immediately to the states. I had such a wonderful experience after that illness. I was in the right place there in Brazil, and the Lord let me stay. Thanks for not writing the letter."

Just as the Holy Ghost may sometimes give us the words to speak, He may also refrain from giving us words because the time isn't right.

GUIDANCE

12

Coincidence is often the Lord working anonymously.

—Unknown

Sherm and I had three small children when he decided to close his law office in Idaho and join a law firm in Utah. We purchased a piece of property in Fruit Heights and were planning to build a house on it, but we needed a place to stay while we built that house. But with three small children it was difficult to find a short-term rental. We had hunted all over the Kaysville-Layton area but had found nothing. Sherm had to return to Idaho, so we decided that I would stay in the motel and continue the search while he drove back to Idaho to take care of his commitments there.

A motel room gets small pretty quickly when you're trying to entertain a six-year-old, a five-year-old, and a three-year-old.

It was a rather cold spring, and as we went to get into the car my small son caught the edge of his little blue corduroy coat on something and ripped it the entire length of the sleeve and down into the body of the coat. It really left him no warmth. I already felt exasperated with my responsibility to find a place to live when we had looked so earnestly and found nothing. I've never had good health and the responsibility of the three children plus the search for a new home seemed rather overwhelming at the time. To rip out the only coat Steve had on a cold day seemed the final straw.

We went back to the motel room and, on our knees, we prayed for help.

The coat was the first priority. I went to the only store I'd seen in Kaysville that looked like it might have a needle and thread. The people at the dry goods store were very friendly. They asked where I lived and what I was trying to do. I explained everything to them as I bought some needles and blue thread.

"I know a family in our ward who found out just last week they were going overseas for a military assignment," one lady said. "I don't know what they plan to do with their house, but you might check that out." I jotted the address down.

I left the store and went straight to a cute home on the corner of Second East and Second South. I knocked on the door and a lovely lady answered. I told her what I'd heard in the store.

"Come in, come in," was the instant reply. The Spirit was so very strong. "You are just the person we have been looking for. And let me fix that coat."

She went to her sewing machine and repaired the coat, telling me the whole time how delighted she was to have us rent her home. They needed to leave before July 1 and that was about when we needed to be there. Needless to say, the situation was perfect. I remain so thankful for the ripped coat and God's guidance to this house.

Once we were moved into the house in Kaysville, we had a year to get our home built in Fruit Heights. First we discovered that we needed to clear a land easement for the power company. Being an attorney, Sherm could usually do that in about a month. In our case, due to complications and problems, it took three months. Next we found we needed thirty more feet on a gravel driveway in order to qualify for the VA loan. That took some time to resolve. A host of other problems surfaced as well.

While we tried to resolve all those concerns, we worked with a builder and planned our new home. We put earnest money down and chose carpet and drapes. As soon as the loan came through, he would be ready to build.

We were excited and kept checking on the loan. At one point the VA office said the loan was cleared and that the papers had been sent to the bank. But bank officials informed us that they hadn't received them. We worked for three months to locate those papers, but they were nowhere. We were beginning to feel desperate. Our lease would be up in just two months, and the building on our house hadn't even begun.

On the morning of the day the loan clearance was mailed to our home, Sherm received a call to serve as a mission president in São Paulo, Brazil. What a blessing it was that we did not have a hole in the ground, any involved loans, and a partially built home. It would have been difficult to serve our mission in Brazil with those financial obligations hanging over our heads. God certainly watched over us and guided us to the very circumstances that would make it possible for us to serve Him.

GUIDED BY PROMPTINGS TO THE RIGHT PLACE

Sometimes through a series of promptings, feelings, and sometimes even what seems to be coincidence, choices are made and the net result is feeling totally guided by a loving Heavenly Father. At times we recognize these situations only as we look back on them. If we see the hand of the Lord in our lives in the past, we can learn to more accurately see it as we are involved.

President Stephen K. Woodhouse, president of LDS Business College, said that in 1982 he felt prompted to move his family from Denver, Colorado, back to Salt Lake City. The Woodhouses moved, and shortly afterwards, Sister Woodhouse gave birth to a stillborn baby. About this same time Sister Woodhouse's sister unexpectedly died.

"Our extended family went through the grief and sorrow together," Brother Woodhouse related. "From the start to the finish, I can just see the path of my life being laid out" (*Church News*, February 1, 1992, p. 11). He *knew* that the Lord had brought him to Salt Lake to be there at that crucial time of tragedy.

President Woodhouse explained that he had interviewed in California for two positions with large corporations, but he felt unsure about what he should do. He stated: "When we were landing at the Salt Lake Airport [on my way home from the interviews in California], I looked at the beautiful mountains and realized that perhaps I would have an opportunity to fulfill my life's desire of teaching college in a spiritual atmosphere. I told my wife I was going to talk to President Beesley. As soon as I walked in the doors at the college, I knew this was the place I wanted to be."

President Woodhouse didn't feel good about the California offers, but he felt wonderful when he thought about being at LDS Business College. He knew he belonged there as soon as he walked through the doors of the college. He was truly guided by promptings and feelings.

"We Are Fasting for Him Today"

President Monson related an experience he had when he was a mission president in Toronto, Canada. One of their missionaries became very sick and was in the hospital for several weeks. As the doctor considered the nature of the serious and complicated surgery, he advised President Monson that there was a possibility the patient would not survive the surgery.

The parents were contacted and they came to Toronto. The missionary's father and President Monson administered to the young missionary, and gave him a blessing. In the same hospital ward with the missionary were five other men with various illnesses and injuries. On the morning of the missionary's surgery, the nurse came to serve the other men breakfast. When she offered a tray to the first man, he declined.

The nurse was a little surprised; the man had injured his toe when he was mowing the lawn and was in quite good health. She could see no reason why he would not want his breakfast, but she thought the second patient would be happy to have an extra portion. However, he also declined his breakfast.

When all five men refused breakfast, the nurse asked them what was wrong. During their visits they had proven themselves to have hearty appetites, and she couldn't understand why they didn't want to eat this morning.

Then one man replied:

> "You see, bed number three is empty. Our friend is in the operating room under the surgeon's hands. He needs all the help he can get. He is a missionary for his church, and while we have been patients in this ward, he has talked to us about the principles of his church—principles of prayer, of faith, of fasting wherein we call upon the Lord for blessings. . . .We don't know much about the Mormon church, but we have learned a great deal about our friend, and we are fasting for him today."

When the surgery was successfully completed, Elder Monson attempted to pay the doctor, but the doctor refused payment, saying, "Why, it would be dishonest for me to accept a fee. I have never before performed surgery when my hands seemed to be guided by a power that was other than my own. No . . . I wouldn't take a fee for the surgery that Someone on high helped me to perform."

The missionary went home for a few months to rest, then returned to Toronto and completed his mission *(Inspiring Experiences That Build Faith from the Life and Ministry of Thomas S. Monson* [SLC: Deseret Book, 1994], pp. 133-34).

Not only were the hands of the surgeon guided in this experience, but the missionary himself must have felt guidance as he talked with the five men he shared a hospital room with. Certainly God's guidance can change not only our lives, but the lives of those around us.

"I Felt the Savior Guiding Me"

A woman related how she was haunted by the mistakes of her past, and was struggling to make sense of her life. One night when she was particularly troubled, she related how "[her] mind caught hold upon a thrilling thought!" She thought of Alma "as he was 'harrowed up in the memory of his own sins'" and his words: "Now as my mind caught hold upon this thought I cried within my heart: O Jesus, thou Son of God. . . ." (Alma 36:17-18). She said,

> I felt the Savior guiding me back along my "garden path," showing me the talents I had gained through each trial. I knew he was pleased with me for getting up when I had stumbled. I realized how much I had to give to others who might be facing similar experiences. My life was filled with renewed meaning and purpose. (Peggy McFarland and Cheryl Carter, *Becoming Women of Strength* [American Fork, UT: Covenant Communications, 1994], p. 2)

"Buy It"

July 1, 1972, was fast approaching. On that date, our time in Brazil would be over. As the date drew nearer, we attempted to plan for this major move in our life. I was pregnant, and the baby was due at the end of May. We would be returning to the United States with no place to live and five children, including a newborn.

I wrote my mother and asked her to look for a good school and neighborhood and then try to find a home we might be interested in. We planned on looking at any possible homes as soon as we returned.

Our plans are often not God's plans, however. Thankfully, He guides us, though, so we can be blessed. We corresponded with my mother about a variety of possibilities, but nothing worked out. During all this, we were informed that visas for the two new mission presidents and their families (our mission was being split) had not been approved. We were delighted that we could stay in Brazil for a longer period of time. We just didn't know from day to day how long it would be.

Meanwhile, Mom finally found a home she thought we'd be interested in. She told the owner we'd be home July 1, and he'd agreed to wait for our return. Even after our return was postponed, he patiently waited. Finally one night Mom called.

"He can't wait any longer," she told us. "He is going to put it back on the market."

"Let us think about it and we'll call you back in the morning," Sherm told her.

He made it a matter of prayer, and in the morning he called Mom. "Buy it," he said, feeling *guided* by the Lord. How right that home was for us!

Before we had left on our mission, Sherm and I had purchased three pieces of property. Although we had tried to sell the land before heading to Brazil, nobody was interested. Now suddenly, one of the properties sold, providing us enough money for a down payment. Just before we left Brazil in September the second piece of property sold, which gave us money to make some special stops on the way home in Peru, Cusco, and Mexico City. The third piece sold after we were home when we had depleted our funds and had no money to live on. Just as that money was almost gone, Sherm's work picked up and we had what we needed.

Sherm always said the Lord would bless and guide us if we did our best. I have a testimony that while He often leaves us to the last hour, He has promised us that His guidance and blessings will come to us.

A VOICE   13

"I have heard that voice a good many times in my life."

—Joseph F. Smith

Bryant S. Hinckley related an incident that occurred as he and Joseph F. Smith were returning from an eastern trip. They traveled by train. At one point, just east of the Green River, Brother Hinckley saw President Smith go to the end of the car and step out onto the platform. Within an instant, he returned and then paused before sitting down just ahead of Elder Hinckley. At that moment the train jerked. Apparently "a broken rail had been the means of ditching the engine and had thrown most of the cars off the track. In the sleeper [Brother Hinckley and the others in the car] were shaken up pretty badly, but [their] car remained on the track."

President Smith told Brother Hinckley that "he had gone on the platform, when he heard a voice saying, 'Go in and sit down.' . . . As he came in and stood in the aisle he thought, 'Oh pshaw, perhaps it is only my imagination'; when he heard the voice again, 'Sit down,' and he immediately took his seat. . . . He, no doubt, would have been seriously injured had he remained on the platform of that car, as the cars were all jammed up together pretty badly. He said, 'I have heard that voice a good many times in my life, and I have always profited by obeying it'" (*The Faith of Our Pioneer Fathers* [SLC: Deseret Book, 1956], pp. 61-62).

THE STILL SMALL VOICE

Patricia R. Roper described how the Spirit protected her family when their house caught fire in the middle of the night. Her husband, Bruce, woke up and directed her to get the children to safety, and he began making telephone calls. Later Patricia's husband asked if she had told him to get up when she had smelled the smoke.

"No," she said, "why?"

"I just heard my name, and that's what woke me up."

When she heard this, Patricia said, "a shiver ran down my spine." To me, that is the Holy Ghost bearing witness through a tingling sensation. Patricia realized the Lord had protected her family from great harm through the whisperings of the still, small voice (*Church News,* August 17, 1991, p. 11).

When Anne Osborn Poelman, the wife of Elder Ronald E. Poelman, first attended a sacrament meeting as a nonmember, she was surprised by the noisy laughing children and the lack of crosses or candles. She found the music and talks moving; even the passing of the sacrament touched her heart. "Filled with conflicting feelings and embarrassed at this unexpected rush of raw emotion, I was seized by an intense desire to escape. . . . I stood up suddenly and ran out of the back door to the parking lot. . . . And stopped. A voice inside my mind said, as clearly and distinctly as if it were an auditory experience, 'Anne, turn around and go back!'" (*The Simeon Solution* [SLC: Deseret Book, 1995], p. 53).

"There's the Light"

Sometimes we think that only deeply spiritual Church leaders are worthy enough to hear the voice of the Spirit. But there are many, many stories from people of all ages, from all walks of life, who have received guidance, protection, and comfort from the still, small voice of the Spirit.

A young women in my Sunday School class told me her experience when she had gone with a friend and her friend's family to Lake Powell on an outing. One night a storm started to come in, and the waves on the lake started to get bigger. The group had two boats, and the group on one boat set up a campsite, only to realize that the group in the second boat did not know where they had docked. So a few of them headed back out on the lake to find their friends.

Because it was getting dark they put a light out so that they could find their way back to camp. It didn't take them too long to find the second boat, but when they tried to find their camp, they couldn't. They drove around and around looking for the light. Darkness came, and large waves were splashing water into both boats. It was cold, and the wind was noisy; they had to yell to hear one another, even though they were sitting side by side. The smaller children began to cry, and nobody knew where to go. They found themselves driving around in circles looking for the light that marked the location of their camp.

Finally they pulled the two boats together and asked the Lord for help. They were really scared. "When we finished the prayer, the boats pulled apart and started off," said the young lady in my Sunday School class. "I was sitting at the back of the boat on one side and my friend was sitting next to me. All of a sudden, I heard a voice say, "Turn around. There's the light.'"

She turned around, and there was the light. She scurried up to the driver and yelled, "The light is behind us!" At first he didn't believe her because they'd just been going that direction. Finally he turned, and there was the light.

Both boats got to shore safely. "When you saw the light, why did you tell me instead of the driver?" this girl asked her friend.

"I never saw any light," her friend replied. Only then did this young woman recognize the source of the help.

Trust in the Lord

Diane Bills relates in her book, *Trust in the Lord,* how she prayed to know if she should marry the young man she was dating. However, instead of the peace she hoped she would feel, she felt confusion and turmoil. Perhaps she hadn't prayed long enough or hard enough, she thought, but when she asked again, the feelings did not change.

Only when she reversed her decision and prayed did she feel the peace she was looking for, but it was not the answer she wanted. She said, "I began almost begging Heavenly Father to help me feel peaceful inside about marrying [this young man]. At that moment a wonderful thing happened. Words began to flow freely into my mind. . . . I understood the words and the message. The voice said, 'Trust in the Lord with all thine heart; and lean not unto thine own understanding. In all thy ways acknowledge him, and he shall direct thy paths' (Proverbs 3:5-6)."

Nevertheless, as the days passed, Diane found that she was still struggling with the answer she had received. She knew that Elder Thomas S. Monson would be speaking at her stake conference on Sunday and she fasted and prayed in order to be in tune with the Spirit.

Her family was able to sit close to the front where they could feel Elder Monson's warmth and love. Diane especially felt his warmth as well as that of the Spirit, a feeling that intensified when Elder Monson began to speak. He said, "I came today with a talk I had prepared to give to you. [He had given it in the morning session.] But as I have sat here in this session, the Spirit has whispered to me to give you a different message, and so, humbly, I do." Elder Monson took his text from Proverbs 3:5-6, the same scripture Diane had heard in her mind when she had prayed to know what she should do.

Diane concludes, "Elder Monson was unaware of the young twenty-one-year-old woman sitting back five or six rows, with her head bowed and tears flowing freely down her cheeks. I felt as though the Lord were speaking directly through him to me" *(Trust in the Lord* [American Fork, Utah: Covenant Communications, 1996], pp. 18-21).

"DON'T SHOOT"

In Seattle, Washington, Police Officer Calvin Rowley was on duty. Not many minutes after a robbery was reported, he saw an orange Volkswagen that had been identified in the robbery as well as several other recent holdups. He and his partner parked some distance from the car and waited. After a few hours two people got into the car and drove away. As the two police officers followed the Volkswagen, Office Rowley radioed for backup.

A plainclothes unit soon appeared behind them, then passed the police car in order to pull ahead of the Volkswagen. It quickly stopped, forcing the Volkswagen to do the same, and two police officers jumped out, weapons raised and pointing at the Volkswagen. Officer Rowley and his partner pulled up behind the car, and both jumped out with their weapons also raised. At that moment Officer Rowley saw a glint of metal inside the car. As he prepared himself to shoot in self-defense, he heard "a calm but authoritative voice say *Don't shoot!*"

After he had backed away out of the line of fire, he saw that what had appeared to be a gun was only the buckle of a seat belt. When he ran to the car and opened the door, he found two frightened, unarmed girls in the car. The girls had seen the police car behind them and the plainclothes backup police in front of them and, thinking they were in the middle of a "cops-and-robbers shootout," they had ducked.

The police discovered that the girls had lent the car to their boyfriends, who had just returned it. The young men were later arrested ("The Line of Fire," *Ensign*, October 1997, p. 66-67).

"Drive Toward the Mailbox"

I've always heard and read about people throughout Church history, including the prophets, who heard a voice. I never expected to have that experience, but now I too can bear personal testimony that it does happen.

On a winter day one of my children called me from school. He'd left an assignment at home that had to be handed in that day. Not only did it need to be handed in that day, but it had to be in before the end of the class period. I didn't have much time.

I grabbed the assignment and dashed for the front door. I had other things on my mind as I sped toward school. All of a sudden I realized that I was going forty-five miles an hour down a street that not only had a twenty-five-mile-an-hour speed limit, but also was covered with a solid sheet of ice. Just ahead of me as the road swerved slightly to the left, a huge repair truck was parked, blocking more than half the road.

I braked immediately and realized that I really had no control as I slid sideways at a pretty good pace. A car was coming up the street with some degree of speed in order to make the incline on the ice. He was passing the truck. I was moving sideways toward the car and truck. The point of impact was inevitable; I was going to hit both the car and truck.

I had no time to think of a strategy, but I distinctly heard the words, "Take your foot off the brake and drive toward the mailbox." I did it instinctively.

As I headed for the mailbox the wheels grabbed just a bit. The other car slipped through the fraction of space left between my car and the truck. I swerved and cleared the truck, finally coming to a stop further down the street at the stop sign.

I remember seeing the workman's face as I passed. It was a look of utter shock. I know he thought he was going to see a rather bad accident. I sat in my car, shaking. When I finally calmed down, I wondered, "What did I hear?"

It was a male voice, soft and firm, although unfamiliar. I have thought about it and even tried to explain it away as "just a thought." But it was more than that. I am so grateful for the Lord's guidance at a difficult time and for the ongoing knowledge I have that God lives, watches over us, and helps us at times even when we do not deserve it.

THEY WERE GIVEN MY NAME

A seminary instructor in Los Angeles, California, Vilma had come to the Church Education Symposium at BYU with her friend Carma. After a week of instruction, the two women were exhausted and ready to go home Friday evening. However, when they got to the airport, there were no longer any seats available on any flight to Los Angeles until Monday. As if that wasn't frustrating enough, they couldn't find any hotel or motel with any vacancies for the weekend. Because of the Church Education Symposium, BYU graduation, Education Week, and a large convention in Salt Lake City, there were simply no hotel accommodations anywhere.

It was five o'clock Friday evening, and Vilma and Carma didn't know what to do. They had already decided they would have to sleep in the airport, since they had no family or friends in Utah. I had met Vilma earlier that summer during a trip to Israel with about sixty church educators, but we didn't know each other really well. The group had traveled on two buses, and Vilma and I had been assigned to the same bus.

As Vilma tried desperately to remember if anyone she had met on the trip lived in the area, she couldn't come up with a single name. The group had come from all over the U.S. as well as Canada, and Vilma realized that she couldn't remember where anyone was from anyway.

Not knowing what else to do, Vilma decided to go to the temple before returning to the airport to spend the night. Suddenly, in the middle of the temple session, Vilma heard a voice say, "JoAnn Hamilton."

When the session was over, she called Information and asked for the phone number for a JoAnn Hamilton. (I like to say that the miracle involved is that I was even home!) When I got her call, I picked them up and brought them to my home for the weekend. We had a great time.

"I Heard the Words Clearly"

One evening Cheryl Carter was sleeping deeply when she awoke suddenly, "feeling strongly impressed to get down on [her] knees and pray concerning a matter." She said,

> As I finished praying, I seemed to hear the words, "Sweet peace be unto thee, dear daughter," and a feeling of love and serenity swept over me. Then, as I lay back down in bed, these two admonitions repeatedly and forcefully came to mind: "Pray always that ye enter not into temptations, lest the evil one have power over thee," and "Pray always that ye strive to do evil no more, but to do good continually."

An instant later, Cheryl said, "I seemed to have a bright recollection of many things of which I had not repented. . . . So vivid was the memory of these events that I could not bear it. . . . I got down on my knees and promised the Lord that I would do all that was necessary to make restitution for these past mistakes."

One incident in particular stood out in her mind, and she determined to seek forgiveness of the person she had offended. The phone call was made, and forgiveness was sought and received. Cheryl said,

Now that she had forgiven me, I needed to know if the Lord would forgive me. Suddenly, I felt a burning in my bosom and a sweet peace came over me as I heard the words just as clearly as if the Savior himself had been standing there, "Thy sins are forgiven. Go thy way and sin no more." Tears of gratitude for my Savior and his eternal sacrifice for me ran down my face. For me, his atonement had truly been realized again. (Peggy McFarland and Cheryl Carter, *Becoming Women of Strength* [American Fork, UT: Covenant Communications, 1994], p. 36)

"DON'T GET IN THE CAR"

Not long ago I met a young woman in another state. She was just coming back to church and told me her story. As an eighteen-year-old, she felt no closeness or acceptance in the ward, so she sought it elsewhere. She drifted from the Church. She lived with different boyfriends, occasionally returning to live with her family where her activities created tension in the home. At one point she ended up in another state, far from Utah. One night she was out with friends who had been drinking, although she had not. She said, "We were going to take off in the car and I heard this voice say, 'Don't get in the car.' I heard it three times." She got into the car anyway. The road was narrow, the area was mountainous. The car went out of control. That it didn't go over the cliff was itself a miracle. She was catapulted from the car and badly hurt.

She decided there had to be a reason she was still alive. "I started looking at myself and my friends. Some had committed suicide; some had died. I decided I didn't want to end up where they were. But it's hard to change."

As we talked, this young woman said to me, "When I was eighteen I just wanted life fun and easy. What I've learned over the last five years is that that lifestyle isn't fun and it isn't easy."

"You Need to Pray"

A young man I'll call Thad also told me his story. At eighteen, he didn't know what direction he wanted to go. Then he got a job playing the saxophone in a band. He had always wanted to play his saxophone in a band and here was the opportunity to do so. He had been thinking about a mission, but only because he couldn't think of anything better to do with his time. Suddenly, here was an option that seemed better. The fact that he was one week away from being ordained an elder didn't really matter. The same week that the opportunity to play in a band arose, he was able to get another job. It didn't seem to matter that he had to work on Sunday. Up to that time, Thad had been thinking and at least talking about going on a mission. He quickly lost interest.

The band was pretty successful. They cut a CD and did a lot of touring. Because everyone in the band used drugs it wasn't long before Thad started, first with marijuana and then he went on to pretty much everything else. As he said, "Sex, drugs, and rock and roll all go together."

Three and half years later he found himself in a bar. Although he'd had a drink, he felt fairly clear-headed. He told me what happened to him there.

> All of a sudden my movement was restricted. I could only move slowly. I couldn't speak. Like a broken record I heard the words in my mind: *You need to pray.* The words repeated themselves over and over. I hoped they would go away. It felt like a living nightmare. It was like this big, old black thing utterly enveloped me. I saw a picture in my mind [as if] I could perceive what the eternal consequences of my actions would be. There was an intense feeling of darkness.

The thought kept coming, *You need to pray.* I went out into the parking lot and knelt down. At that point I could finally speak. It was like a communication of feelings but I knew what was being said. I felt like it was a loving reprimand. I knew then that my parents loved me. I knew that I had been taught and that the Lord was disappointed in me, but that I had a work to do. Words cannot describe what I went through.

From that point I decided to pursue whatever the Lord wanted me to do. In order to do that I had to break off all my relations. I was so totally alone.

This young man acknowledged to me his appreciation for lots of loving support from his parents. No, it wasn't an exact voice he heard, but the message was unmistakable. He turned his life around and decided to prepare for a mission. Not long ago, he received his call. How does he feel about it? "Wonderful!"

"Almost Like a Voice"

Sometimes people hear a voice very clearly, and other times they say the words come as clearly as if it were a voice. Either way, the feeling is just as powerful. One young man told how the Spirit comforted him and his wife when she experienced a miscarriage. He was praying for understanding one day as he was driving to work and the answer came quietly but surely. "It was as if a voice had said to me, 'I didn't want you to lose that baby, but it just has to be this way. I hurt as badly as you do. . . .' From that point on, I could learn to deal with the loss because I knew that Heavenly Father loved us and understood our pain. I could turn away from anger and blame, and concentrate on the healing process in a more positive manner" (Sherri Devashrayee Wittwer,

Gone Too Soon: The Life and Loss of Infants and Unborn Children [American Fork, UT: Covenant Communications, 1994], p. 86).

After adopting a son, one sister was considering a second adoption so he would not be raised as an only child. When she heard that people were going to Romania to adopt the orphaned children there, she was interested but hesitant. She was overwhelmed by the idea of choosing one child when there were so many in need. The "breakthrough" came when she was writing in her journal, and she described how Heavenly Father taught her through the voice of His Spirit:

> These are Father's children. They are His. I can trust Him to set things right. If not in this life, then when they pass through the veil. I am only one person: I can only do what I can do. If that is only to love one of those children, then I'll do it! Then, almost like a voice, a message came directly to me from my Heavenly Father: "Jeanna, if you're willing, I could use you." (DeAnna and Terry Ball, eds., *Each One a Miracle: Inspirational Romanian Adoption Stories* [Orem, UT: Grandin Book Co., 1994], pp. 43-44)

ANSWERS THROUGH OTHERS 14

"God watches over us and loves us, but it is usually through another person that he meets our needs."

—*Spencer W. Kimball*

Sherm and I had an elder in our mission who, after he had been in Brazil for one week, came to the mission home with his baggage and told us that he had now seen enough of Brazil. He was ready to go home. My husband interviewed Elder Simpson and found that he was the only one in his family who had joined the Church. It wasn't hard for Sherm to figure out that if he sent Elder Simpson home, his family would say, "I told you so." He'd probably be embarrassed at church and might stop attending his meetings and become inactive.

We loved this young man too much to let that happen if we could avoid it. Sherm was able to talk Elder Simpson into staying just a little longer, and then assigned him to an area near the mission home so they could have frequent, regular interviews. He also gave him a very special companion.

Through frequent, encouraging interviews, we thought we might be able to keep Elder Simpson on his mission for just six months, then he would be over the hump and wouldn't want to leave. However, as we neared the time when our mission was over, we felt genuine concern that the new mission president would listen to Elder Simpson once and simply send him back to the states.

Our friend Dave Christensen was in Brazil with his family at the time, working to establish the seminary program there. Dave had a great rapport with the elders, and we felt that if Elder Simpson became close to Dave, after we left there would be a tie that would hold him that last little bit until he loved his mission and wouldn't want to leave. Dave agreed to work with Elder Simpson.

One day Elder Simpson came in for his interview. Although Sherm had planned on the interview, he was detained. Normally missionaries would just wait until Sherm arrived. On this day, however, I was in the office when Elder Simpson came in. I *knew* I was to talk to him and arrange for him to meet Dave Christensen. Knowing my husband as I did, I knew he would understand. I invited Elder Simpson into my office, then sent the mission secretary to find Dave with a request to come to my office.

This was one of those choice experiences when I just *knew* what to do. I sat down with Elder Simpson and drew a vertical line that veered upward. We talked about where he was now and where he would be if he completed his mission.

I drew another line and angled it down. We talked about where his life would go if he chose to go home early. Then I had no more to say. At that moment, there was a knock on the door, and there was Brother Christensen. I introduced them, showed him what we had been talking about, and left.

As I left my office I was filled with joy, another feeling the Holy Ghost uses in order to communicate. I *knew* I had done right. Just then the mission secretary came running up the stairs.

"Sister Hibbert, Sister Hibbert," he said. "I couldn't find Brother Christensen anywhere."

Later I asked Dave why he had come to my office. "I was looking for my children," he said, "and *felt* like you needed me."

Elder Simpson finished his mission in Brazil. Years later he drove all the way from California to Utah to give Sherm and me and Brother Christensen a hug. Elder Simpson had been married in the temple, had two little children, and was mission leader in his ward. He was so grateful that we had encouraged him to finish his mission and provided a way for him to feel the love and support he needed. But we knew we had only done what the Lord had wanted us to do.

AN ANGEL OR STEVE

President Kimball has said, "God watches over us and loves us, but it is usually through another person that he meets our needs" (*Ensign*, December 1974, p. 2).

My son Steve and a group of his friends who were all young scouts went down to southern Utah for a camping trip. Originally the boys and Carl, the group's leader, had planned to join up with another car that had left earlier. But in an attempt to catch up to the first car, Carl and his scouts had taken a shortcut. Now short-cuts are not always what they seem to be, and they found that the unpaved road had many curves and actually took longer than the original route. Darkness descended, so the group decided to camp where they were out there in the mountains.

Now scouts being scouts, they stayed up very late that night. Carl headed to bed a bit earlier than the boys, and consequently got up earlier the next morning. He found the young men still sleeping, and so, loving the mountains as he did, Carl decided to hike around a bit. It was beautiful and he had a glorious time wandering around appreciating nature. However, when he decided to return to camp, he quickly discovered he'd lost his way. He had had a stroke some months earlier and at times the aftereffects still left him somewhat disoriented.

"There are prayers and there are prayers," said Carl, as he related this experience. "There are the kind of prayers you ask at night by your bed when you are really sleepy and in a hurry and the kind you ask when you are in the mountains and can't find your Scouts and you are the only driver.

"That was the one time in my life when I prayed for an angel. I needed one to show me the way."

And then he said with a smile, "I guess the Lord doesn't need to send an angel if He can send a Steve."

My tall and lanky son had awakened early that morning. Now I want you to know that my boy *never* wakes up early, but this morning he did. Then he, too, decided to go on a hike, and he took exactly the same hike that Carl took. Just as Carl was getting off his knees, he heard a noise coming through the leaves. It was my son, who remembered the way back to the boys. The Lord had answered a prayer in the form of another person.

The Cupboard Was Bare

My husband Sherm and his companion were the only missionaries in an area far from the mission home. They received letters and packages sporadically; mail service in Brazil was far from dependable. However, it was the only method missionaries had to receive their monthly money.

In December these two elders went days and then weeks without receiving mail or packages. Although Christmas presents would have been nice, they were even more concerned about their money as they were quickly running out of it.

When the two young men ran out of money, they just started eating whatever was left in the kitchen cupboards. Eventually, however, the cupboard was bare.

There was no mail or food the day before Christmas, and these two missionaries had eaten their last meal that morning. They returned from the post office, knowing there would be no mail the next day and wondering how they would manage.

Two hungry elders woke up Christmas morning to find a huge basket of food on their doorstep. There was no name on it, but it was not hard to figure out who in the small branch had left it. They knew immediately it had come from a particular caring ward member who probably had no idea how desperately it was needed. The food in that basket sustained those elders until their money arrived several days later.

Fourteen years later when my husband returned to Brazil to serve as a mission president, this same brother came to welcome Sherm back. Sherm invited him into his office, and then asked, "Do you remember that basket of food you left on our doorstep all those years ago on Christmas morning?"

The man remembered.

Sherm then asked him if he realized how badly the two elders had needed it. He did not.

"Have you ever left baskets like that on other elders' doorsteps?" Sherm asked. He had not. The Lord so often works through other people to take care of His own.

THE LORD PLACED HIM IN MY LIFE

As John considered his life, he wondered if he should end it all. This was not the first time he had thought about suicide, but he had been able to talk himself out of it before. He explained later, "I had gone through so much pain, sorrow, and continual downfall that I thought there was no hope for me. I tried to come up with options but felt like I had none. It had been a long three years since I had left my family, my friends, and the Church. Suicide seemed my only way out."

As he was thinking, John placed an unlabeled cassette in his stereo player and was startled to hear the words from the song: "Will he answer me? Does he really hear my prayers?" The thought remained with him all night and at last he sought relief in prayer, something he hadn't done for a long time. The thought that God did hear his prayers brought him some comfort and peace. The next morning he decided he would go to church the next weekend.

John sat near the back of the chapel, feeling awkward and alone. "I sat there thinking this was a stupid idea," he said, and got up to leave, determined to put an end to his life.

"As I was leaving, a young man about my age introduced himself to me as Steve. He said he was living with his aunt and uncle and working to earn money to go on a mission. He was very friendly, but I did not feel at ease." The young man excused himself briefly and returned with an invitation to come to his house for dinner so they could get to know each other better.

John found Steve's aunt and uncle to be very friendly, and he felt their concern for him. "I can't explain what it felt like to be loved again," he said. "For three years I had turned my back on everything I had loved. Everything in my life had gone wrong. But now, suddenly, I felt new life. My Heavenly Father had answered my prayer in the form of a young man preparing to go on a mission, his aunt and uncle, and their family. . . . The Lord had placed him in my life just long enough to help me get back on my feet again in the Church" ("The Ripple Effect," in Michele Garvin, ed., *By Small and Simple Things* [American Fork, UT: Covenant Communications, 1996], pp. 39-42).

"GOD KNEW SHE NEEDED HELP"

I love to talk to people, as did my visiting teaching companion. We knew that sometimes we spent far too long visiting with the sweet sisters we were assigned. One particular month, my companion and I decided that for once we would stay on the lesson and not stay so long. I seriously committed, we had prayer, and then we entered the door for the visit.

A few minutes into that visit I mentioned a health problem one of my children had. Although my companion and I had both made a firm decision to keep our visits short, I felt very strongly about what I was saying, and our visit grew quite lengthy. I really felt stupid as we left that day, and I apologized profusely to my companion for talking so much and especially for talking about a health problem that had obviously not been on the lesson at all.

As I entered my house after that visit the phone was ringing. The sister we had just visited was calling. "I didn't want to say more while you were here but I think my daughter has the same health problem," she said. She had more questions for me, and I was able to address some of her concerns.

"SOMEONE IS TELLING YOU TO DO YOUR DUTY"

When Elder Harold B. Lee attended a special testimony meeting for stake presidents in the Salt Lake Temple, he was so moved by one man's testimony that he recorded it later and kept it in his files. President Ballantyne of the Southern Arizona Stake told about his childhood in Star Valley, Wyoming, and his family's struggle to make ends meet. His father often had to work for some of the large ranchers for about a dollar a day, which was barely enough to take care of himself, let alone send any home to his wife and children. Said President Ballantyne,

> We had our family prayers around the table, and it was one such night that Father was gone that we gathered, and Mother poured out of a pitcher into a glass for each one, milk divided among the children, but none for herself. And I, sensing the fact that the milk in the pitcher was all that we had, pushed mine over to Mother and said, "Mother, you drink mine."

Although she told him she wasn't hungry and insisted that her son drink his milk, he was so worried that he couldn't sleep. He finally left his bed and tiptoed down the stairs, "and there was Mother out in the middle of the floor kneeling in prayer. . . . I heard her say, 'Heavenly Father, there is no food in our house today. Please, Father, touch the heart of somebody so the children will not be hungry in the morning.'"

The next morning the children were awakened by "the sound of pots and pans in the kitchen and the smell of cooking food."

"Mother, I thought you said there was not any food," he said.

"Well, my boy," was her reply, "didn't you think the Lord would answer my prayer?"

"Years passed," said President Ballantyne, "and I went away to college. I was married and I came back now to see the old folks. Old Bishop Gardner was now reaching up to a ripe old age, but he still had a keen memory." He told President Ballantyne how he had been home one night, reading the paper.

My shoes were off and I was sitting by the fireplace. I heard a voice that said, "Sister Ballantyne doesn't have any food." I thought it was my wife. I called out, "What did you say, Mother?"

She came in wiping her hands on a towel and asked, "Did you call me, Father?"

"No, I didn't say anything, but somebody did."

"What did they say?" she asked.

"It said that Sister Ballantyne didn't have any food in her house."

"Well then," she said, "you better put on your shoes and your coat and go over and take some food to Sister Ballantyne. Somebody is telling you to do your duty as a bishop."

That night, Bishop Gardner took meat, flour, and all the necessities and left it outside of the Ballantyne home in the dark. Elder Lee concluded, "We have the right to that kind of spiritual direction, if we live for it" (L. Brent Goates, *Modern-Day Miracles from the Files of President Harold B. Lee* [American Fork, UT: Covenant Communications, 1996], pp. 131-33).

MISSED PROMPTINGS AND OTHER OBSTACLES

15

"Never postpone a prompting of the Spirit."

—*Thomas S. Monson*

As we struggle to learn to identify promptings, often it is easy to notice at first when we miss one. We find ourselves saying, "I had a feeling I should have done that!" We don't need to spend a lot of time wallowing in guilt; the important thing is to learn from the experience.

So often, we're simply caught up in doing things. I remember doing dishes over my kitchen sink and having wonderful ideas for a family home evening lesson. Not recognizing the source at the time, I wrote the thoughts down and put them in a family home evening file—which I never took time to refer to. The Lord tried so hard to help me; I simply didn't understand how he was trying to help me.

President Thomas S. Monson shares a time when he learned this important lesson.

> One evening in 1951, when I served as bishop of the Sixth-Seventh Ward, I received a telephone call from a former schoolmate of mine at the University of Utah. He advised me that his uncle, Brother Brown, was seriously ill in the Veterans Hospital. Since Brother Brown lived in my ward, although inactive, his nephew asked if I would find time to go to the hospital and give him a blessing. This I agreed to do.
>
> On that particular night, we had our stake priesthood meeting, followed by stake priesthood leadership meeting. My obligation was clear. I would attend my meetings and then visit the hospital.
>
> I found it extremely difficult to sit through the first meeting, for I felt strongly that I should be at the Veterans Hospital at the side of Brother Brown. When the first meeting adjourned, I told my counselors to kindly excuse me from the second meeting—that I must go to the hospital, which I did.
>
> When I arrived at the hospital, I rushed to the information desk and ascertained the number of Brother Brown's room. Not waiting for the elevator, I ran upstairs.
>
> I arrived at his room just as the attending doctor pulled the sheet over his face. The nurse said, "Could you be Bishop Monson?"

"Yes, ma'am," I replied.

She said, "He was calling your name when he died."

I left the hospital with a determination in my heart that when conflicts of duty appear, an essential visit must take precedence over a scheduled meeting. I learned also this truth: *Never postpone a prompting of the Spirit. (Inspiring Experiences That Build Faith from the Life and Ministry of Thomas S. Monson* [SLC: Deseret Book, 1994], p. 18; emphasis in original)

"I'll Go Monday"

I had a similar heartbreaking experience, one that I will never forget. I had a neighbor whom I loved very much. Connie had kids the same age as my older children and had lived close to us for many years. Then she and her family moved out of the area for a period of time. I was thrilled when they returned to our neighborhood.

In time Connie found that she had a brain tumor, and we all knew that eventually we were going to lose her. I went to visit her and tell her of my love and concern; we had such a choice conversation.

About three weeks later I had a recurring thought all week that I should go and visit Connie again. I was busy that week. I had lots of things listed in my day planner that I thought I needed to do. But the thought kept coming. Every morning I'd write her name in my planner on a list of things to do that day; the next morning I'd write her name down again. I just kept moving it each day. Finally I said to myself, "Okay, I'll go for sure on Monday."

Connie passed away over that weekend. Everyone in the ward, including myself, thought she had another three or four months. God knew better. I still feel bad that I didn't listen.

AFRAID TO LISTEN

Even when I recognize a prompting as coming from the Lord, I sometimes lack the faith to go with God. Because of my own lack of perspective or my own personal fears, I hesitate.

As a mission president, Sherm always wanted to improve mission conferences. So following each conference we'd ask the missionaries to list two things they liked about the conference and two things we could improve on.

As is tradition, as part of the mission conferences I usually spoke. The missionaries often mentioned my talk on their slips of paper under the "things we like about mission conference" category. I have to admit, I was feeling pretty good about that particular talk.

The last mission conference was in Curitiba. I had a newborn baby girl, and because I was taking care of her, I arrived late to the meeting. As I entered the room I had a distinct thought enter my mind that I should give my talk on a different subject.

Unfortunately I occasionally find myself almost arguing with the Lord. This was one of those occasion. "I can't give a talk on that," I told Him. "I'm not prepared." I sat down, and within minutes, Sherm called on me to speak. In my weakness I stood and gave the same talk I had given in the other conferences. As soon as I started I realized what I was doing. It was the worst talk I have ever given because it was the wrong talk. After it was over I slipped into a classroom next door and apologized to the Lord. "I ask for your help, and then when you give it to me I don't listen," I said humbly. "I'm so sorry."

A week or so later I attended a district meeting. Somehow I knew there was a problem in that district, but I didn't know what the problem was. I went prepared with a talk, but as I entered the room I felt I should talk on a different subject. This time I obeyed those promptings, and to my amazement helped to solve the problem.

CALL THEM AND LET THEM KNOW

Another time I missed the boat by ignoring the subtle promptings of the Spirit. I wanted to lecture with the Church Educational System's Especially For Youth program and submitted an application. When I didn't get a reply before Christmas, I assumed I had been turned down. Then, to my surprise, I received a letter asking me to submit four outlines for the Church correlation committee to check in consideration for use by the EFY Program. Nevertheless, the letter said that submission of these materials would in no way assure me of a spot on the program. I submitted the outlines, but again received no reply. Time passed and I just assumed I had not been accepted.

Several weeks after I had submitted my outlines, I was busy preparing for a trip to Bellingham, Washington, where I had been invited to speak to a group of youth in one meeting and a group of sisters in a stake Relief Society meeting. It was a busy, hectic week because of everything I was involved with—daily seminary preparation, apartment management responsibilities, family responsibilities, and so on. When I returned from Washington I would be getting ready to take a trip to the Holy Land because my husband and I had signed up to go with other part-time seminary teachers.

I should have recognized the persistent, recurring thought that I had that week. It probably came five or six times: "You really ought to call the people involved with the EFY program and tell them that you have committed to go to Israel June 12 through July 2, so that if you are accepted you will not be scheduled during that time."

But busy with preparations for my trip to Washington, I listened to the argument of my logical self. "You probably didn't get accepted anyway. What makes you think you are good enough for them? Besides, you'll have more time next week. You can call them then."

When I returned from Washington, there in the mail was a letter from the Church Educational System. I had been accepted to give two talks at Academy for Boys and Academy for Girls—during the time I would be in Israel. The letter was very clear. There would be no rescheduling. God had been trying to get me into the program. It was me who missed the prompting.

Beware of Logic

Just before my son Dan entered the Missionary Training Center, our family had a special home evening with him, spending some time on our very old boat and our little ski bob. We had enjoyed this many times before, and we always had lots of fun together.

Dan was on the ski bob, enjoying himself. The water was choppy, which made it even more fun. All of a sudden, the thought entered his mind that he should let go of the rope. His logic said, "That's stupid. I'm having a good time!"

Just then the rope around the front of the ski bob slipped and caught my missionary son around his arm, flipping his six-foot-nine-inch body down into the water and pulling him down by his arm underneath the water. No one saw it happen. Dan thought he was going to drown before the others noticed what was happening and stopped the boat. When I saw him a few minutes later, his arm hung limp at his side and his hand was blue.

We raced for ice and a doctor. As it turned out, he entered the MTC a very blessed young man. He could have lost his life or his right arm so easily. He still wears the mark of the rope around that arm.

My son was blessed. Even though he didn't act on that prompting, God preserved his arm and hand. We are so grateful.

I remember a number of years ago when there were more apartments in Salt Lake than there were renters. After my first husband's death, I had purchased a number of apartments with the insurance money. In order to stay solvent financially, my second husband and I had to keep our apartments rented. Vacancies really hurt us.

At one point we had a vacancy for a couple of weeks. This was a major concern. Finally a young couple who were expecting their first child looked at the apartment. They really liked it. The only problem was that the husband had no work, they had no savings, and she had only part-time work. Logically they were not the right renters. Even though we needed the apartment filled, filling it with a family who couldn't pay rent didn't help us at all.

I took an application from them anyway, headed home, and talked the situation over with my husband Fred and my children. We had already learned through sad experience that when a sweet young couple who lived in our apartments couldn't pay the rent, I could never kick them out. We had financial obligations to meet in order to stay solvent, I reminded myself. We just couldn't afford to have tenants who couldn't pay rent. This couple certainly didn't seem to fit into the category of as acceptable residents for us. We all agreed that renting to them wouldn't be the logical decision. It was better to leave it empty for a while longer and find someone who could really pay the rent than to rent to this couple.

I had asked them to call me back in a couple of days. I dreaded their phone call and the bad news I would have to give them. Finally the phone call came. I knew in my heart it was them. My husband was in the room when I answered the phone.

"Have you decided if we can have the apartment?" the young woman asked.

To my surprise I found myself saying, "Yes, we'd like to have you." As I said this I felt the Spirit very strongly. Those little tingly things went through me, and I felt wonderful.

My husband looked at me with surprise. After I got off the phone I explained how right I felt about it. He understood what I was talking about and said no more.

The couple moved in the next week. "Guess what?" the husband said with a grin when he saw me. "Last week I found a full-time job." The Lord knew all along that the husband would find a job. I was so grateful for the prompting, and just as grateful that I hadn't let my logical self govern my actions.

Some time later, when the rental market was better, several young couples applied to live in one of our apartments. They all could afford the rent, and any one of the couples would be wonderful renters.

However, one couple stood out. They hadn't been the first to see the apartment, and I already had several good applications. Like everyone else, they *really* wanted the apartment.

These two had been married for five years. He was a returned missionary, and they had married in the temple. After they married, he was diagnosed with diabetes; he had had a kidney removed and was nearly blind. The couple had two children, and he was able to provide some care for the children while his wife went to school to gain a vocation so she could support the family.

Given the situation, they were not the logical renters for a landlord who wanted an easy and convenient situation. But as I talked to them I felt the Spirit and I knew the Lord wanted them there.

I rented to them. At the time I did not know that in that ward was another young couple with a situation like theirs, only just the opposite. Now how many wards in Bountiful have couples where one of the couple is blind? Imagine how much support these couples could give one another. It was right to rent to them because God wanted them there.

Taking the Time to Listen

As with other personal revelations from a loving God, thoughts come to us about the little things as well as the big. How important it is that we listen to those thoughts.

When my son Dave was in junior high, his tonsils were taken out. The surgery was scheduled for Friday, and Dave wanted to be back in school on Monday.

The doctor gave his permission as long as Dave took his medication at noon. I can't remember why I didn't send it with him, but I do remember his reminding me to be on time; the tardy policy was extremely strict, and a tardy was almost worse than an absence.

As I was leaving the house to take Dave his pill, the phone rang. I shouldn't have answered it, but I did, which put me behind schedule. Because I was hurrying as I dashed out the front door, I ignored the thought that came into my mind that I should bring a glass of water with me.

"I can just see me driving down Center Street with an elephant pill in one hand and a cup of water in the other," I thought lightheartedly.

Dave was waiting for me when I pulled in the parking lot. Seconds away from being late, the first question he asked was, "Did you bring a cup of water?" No, I had not. And so my son was late to class because I didn't listen to the knowledge the Lord had given me. Certainly, this kind of knowledge won't make a difference in the eternal scheme of things, but it was useful knowledge that would have made a small difference in the life of one boy.

RESPOND TO THE LITTLE NUDGES

The Holy Ghost can communicate with us through feelings that are strong and unmistakable, but it speaks to us with little nudges as well. Too often we ignore these little nudges, telling ourselves that they just don't make sense. Then we learn that the Spirit was trying to help us, even to protect us. A young man in my seminary class shared this experience. He was a fine young man who wanted to keep his mind clean. The night before seminary he had gone to the store and was looking at a computer magazine. As he opened the magazine to a particular page he had a feeling he shouldn't turn the page. But his logical self said, "This is a *computer* magazine, for goodness' sake. There's not going to be anything bad in here." Nevertheless, as soon as he turned the page, he wished he hadn't.

President Kimball warned us, "Expecting the spectacular, one may not be fully alerted to the constant flow of revealed communication" (Edward L. Kimball, ed., *The Teachings of Spencer W. Kimball* [SLC: Bookcraft, 1982], p. 457; emphasis added).

For instance, let's imagine that you are about to sign a contract for the purchase of something. This purchase is significant to you—it may be a car, a home, some equipment for school or work. You have prayed about the purchase and asked for help and guidance. After all, Jesus Christ has told us again and again to ask, and has promised that if we ask, it will be given to us. As you read the contract, you feel a slight feeling of discomfort, and you are tempted to shrug it off as not being very important. But you wait; you listen. You read the contract very carefully. You pray for understanding. And then, as you go back over the contract, you notice a particular paragraph. As you read it again, you feel uncomfortable about the terms listed. So many times this tiny feeling of discomfort is a prompting that, yes, there is a problem.

Let's consider another situation. You are praying every day and asking God to help you. One day as you are writing a family letter, you end with a certain comment. As you reread the letter you feel uncomfortable about the comment. This little niggling concern is a prompting. The uncomfortable feeling is often a suggestion given through the gift of the Holy Ghost that there is indeed a better way to say what you want to say. Or perhaps it is better to not say it at all. As you adjust the letter, you will find something that feels right.

A DIVERSITY OF WAYS   16

"God moves in a mysterious way, his wonders to perform."—William Cowper

I would like to relate a moving and wonderful true story by Dora D. Flack to illustrate the diversity of ways in which God operates to accomplish His will. We see, too, how God responded to His children's requests and how they, in turn, responded to His promptings.

At the Christmas program the Sunday before Christmas, Dale Fonnesbeck was at the organ, accompanying the Kaysville Utah Seventh Ward choir, while his wife, DeAnn, and their five children sat on the front row where they could offer their support. No one had any premonition that certain events in the near future might prevent Dale from performing at the organ ever again.

The next evening Dale was busily engaged in his garage workshop, finishing his Christmas gifts for his children. Since space in their home was sadly lacking, Dale was making sets of drawers to slide under bunk beds.

> [Dale] drew guidelines on a plank, marking dado slots for the drawers. Suddenly he realized that his new dado blade shouldn't be mounted on his circular saw. (A dado blade is shaped like a windmill, with sharp carbide tips on the end of each blade.) He shrugged, knowing he had to use that blade tonight to keep on schedule.

> A strong impression came, warning him not to use the blade. Dale reasoned with himself, promising he'd be careful.

While the Spirit often speaks softly, in times of impending tragedy, the Spirit often sends a much stronger feeling; otherwise we might dismiss a small, uncomfortable nudge. Even so, our reaction, as Dale's was, is so often to use our logic to ignore promptings.

> Holding the saw trigger in his right hand, [Dale] held the plank firmly with his left hand to control vibration. When the saw had cut halfway down the plank, his eyes shifted to the end of the board. In that instant, the saw blade caught the sleeve of his sweatshirt. For some unknown reason, the blade stalled.

> Dale glanced down to see why. The blade had carved a half-inch groove halfway across his hand, between the lower thumb joint and the wrist

joint! Somehow he remained calm and didn't jerk back. Pulling back would release the stalled blade and amputate his hand.

Had the blade not stalled, and had Dale not remained calm—certainly a calm bestowed by the Spirit—Dale's hand would have been amputated immediately. Many times in crisis, God gives us peaceful and calm feelings so that we can do what is necessary.

The amount of blood pumping from his hand told him the main artery was severed. His thumb collapsed in the cut palm of the hand and the index finger hung down over the thumb, both lifeless.

With incredible calm, Dale released the saw from the incision and grabbed his left hand with his right, pressing hard with his thumb against the severed artery. How could there be no pain?

Blessed with calm and relief, Dale was also granted a *knowledge* of what he should do. He hurried back into the house, where the children were sleeping and his wife was reading. It was 9:30 p.m. He calmly informed his wife that he had cut his hand and she would need to call an ambulance. Even though at the time DeAnn didn't realize the extent of the injury, she didn't stop to ask questions but rather, quickly dialed the emergency number. She *knew* she needed to respond with utmost haste.

The dispatcher asked how badly was Dale's hand cut. Because Dale was so calm, she wasn't sure. He replied, "'Halfway through my hand. Tell them to hurry!'

Although DeAnn was now beginning to feel the strain of fear and panic, Dale knew he needed to wrap his hand in a towel and to lay quietly on the floor before he fainted from loss of blood. Again, it is significant that Dale seemed to *know* just what to do. This was the Spirit of the Lord guiding him.

DeAnn telephoned her parents who arrived just as the paramedics did. Her neighbor, Vic Sorensen, also joined them. Vic was also a member of their bishopric. As the paramedics evaluated the situation, Vic and DeAnn's father administered to Dale. They felt "prompted to promise him proper care," an unusual blessing, but one that will become evident as the story continues.

Since Dale obviously needed a hand surgeon, it was decided to airlift him to St. Mark's hospital, which was in Salt Lake City, thirty miles away.

"Coincidentally" the area had been totally fogged in for two weeks, but on that night the fog cleared up. As it has often been said, coincidence is so often the Lord working anonymously.

Although Dale had as yet received no medication for pain, he felt absolutely none. At the hospital, he was immediately prepped for surgery.

Meanwhile, DeAnn, who had left the children with her mother, hurried to the hospital with her father and sat nervously holding his hand. She felt some concern when a man approached her. The heavy, open shoes he wore indicated that he'd undergone some sort of foot surgery, and his eyes were black and blue, as if he'd been in a fight. He introduced himself as the doctor and assured her that he was fine. He'd had surgery and looked terrible, but he would be able to take good care of her husband. DeAnn felt enormous peace and *knew* that Dale would receive the best care possible. She later found out that the surgeon, Dr. John R. Ream, was one of the foremost hand surgeons in the West.

As the Lord was blessing both Dale and DeAnn with peace and the best medical care available, He was blessing them in another way as well. Dale had been promised in his blessing that he would receive "proper medical care" and a neighbor was prompted to assist in a special way.

Back in Kaysville, Joe Gilmore, a neighbor, knew that cleaning up the scene after an accident can be traumatic to the victim's family. He reasoned that was probably the best way he could help. He entered the garage and, noticing there wasn't much blood, recognized that Dale's quick thinking had prevented greater loss of blood.

Before grabbing a broom, Joe searched carefully for anything the paramedics might have overlooked. He discovered bone fragments and called the hospital. When hospital staff assured him that the fragments would be needed in order to reconstruct the bone of Dale's hand, Joe rushed the bone fragments to the hospital.

When Brother Gilmore arrived, the fragments were rushed into surgery and were found to be indispensable in the hand reconstruction, because the bone from the donor bank was not adhering properly. . . .

"As they were working on me," Dale recalls, "I remember thinking that I might have to change my lifestyle. Could I still work as an engineer? Do carpentry? Play the organ?"

After eight hours of surgery, Dale's hand was finally put in a cast. Dale was awake, having received only a local anesthetic. "Is there any movement?" Dale wondered. Very carefully he tried to move his fingertips. They actually moved! "They'll be all right," he sighed, relieved.

Dale was told that his hand would be in the cast for three months, but Dr. Ream found that the cast could be removed in only three weeks. Dale missed only two weeks of work. In time, with therapy, Dale was able to regain almost full use of his hand. He concluded:

> "So many miracles. . . . And I know they all add up to answers to prayers—and blessings because of that priesthood administration. I have asked myself, Why did the dado blade stall instead of completely amputating my hand? Why did I remain so calm so I could seal off the artery? How did Dad get to our house so quickly? Why was Vic there immediately to help administer to me? Why did the fog clear—that night? If Joe hadn't cleaned up the workshop and found bone fragments, my hand would have been damaged permanently. And how blessed I was that Dr. Ream recovered from his own surgeries sufficiently to be on duty that night." (Dora D. Flack, "The Gift of a Hand," *Ensign*, September 1991, pp. 39-41; used by permission)

As this experience shows us, God often helps us in a number of ways, providing a number of feelings, in any one situation where His help is needed.

A WARNING, A CONCLUSION, AND A SURE GUIDE   17

"All people, if they are worthy enough and close enough to the Lord, can have revelations."

—*Spencer W. Kimball*

God is alive and well and He would help us if we let Him. He would have us read the scriptures because in them we can find answers to our problems. They were given to us to be a source of strength as well as knowledge. Our Heavenly Father would have us attend our meetings, go to the temple, give service, heed the words of our leaders, read our Church magazines and in so doing come closer to becoming more like Him. These activities can all provide answers for us. Our Father will also help us on a daily basis through personal revelation.

President Spencer W. Kimball said, "The Lord will give you answer to your questions and to your prayers if you are listening. It doesn't have to all come through the prophet. . . .

But all people, if they are worthy enough and close enough to the Lord, can have revelations" (Edward L. Kimball, ed., *The Teachings of Spencer W. Kimball* [SLC: Bookcraft, 1982], p. 455).

An important thing to remember is that personal revelation never violates what the scriptures teach us or what the prophet says; it never directs us to do things beyond our vested authority or Church calling. President Kimball continued, "If one does receive revelations, which one may expect if he is worthy, they will always be in total alignment with the program of the Church; they will never be counter. And they will always be within his own jurisdiction and never beyond. . . ." "Whenever an individual gets out of his area and begins to tell the bishop of revelations he's received for the conduct of the ward, then he's wrong. His revelations are coming from the wrong source because God is not the author of confusion" (*Ibid.* p. 458, 453).

A Sure Guide

The Book of Mormon gives us direction on how to discern the source of our feelings:

> But behold, that which is of God inviteth and enticeth to do good continually; wherefore, every thing which inviteth and enticeth to do good, and to love God, and to serve him, is inspired of God. . . .

> But whatsoever thing persuadeth men to do evil, and believe not in Christ, and deny him, and serve not God, then ye may know with a perfect knowledge it is of the devil. (Moroni 7:13, 17)

One of our challenges is to decide which are our own emotional feelings, our own personal thoughts and which come from God. I used to think all the really good ideas were mine. I have found as years pass that they come from Him—the wonderful ideas as well as the subtle suggestions and strong feelings that aim me in the right direction. I have found that one thing that helps me to identify the Lord's hand is recording my feelings in my journal and then going back and reading the outcome.

A LOVING FATHER IS WATCHING US

I watched as a man in an orange stocking hat carefully unloaded a four-wheeler out of his trailer. As his excited young son climbed on it and started up a dirt path on the side of the hill, the man's eyes followed his son intently.

I couldn't help but notice that he was dressed a bit on the shabby side. His truck had obviously seen lots of use and the trailer was far from new. The beloved four-wheeler was obviously the result of some degree of sacrifice.

The boy went a short distance and then the four-wheeler got stuck in the sand. Only then did he look back to his father for help. The father hastened to pull him out. As soon as he was released, off the boy went without a backward look. The father's gaze never left his son. Stuck again? Off the father went to help his son.

We are so like this boy. We rush off in our busy lives and only when we are stuck do we seek for help from the One who can really help us. How much wiser we would be to listen as we go. Instead of waiting until our four-wheeler gets stuck in the sand, I pray that we might all look to our loving Father on a daily basis for help and guidance. As we learn to identify the promptings, let us ask for help from God to help us recognize thoughts and urgings and other feelings that are indeed from Him. And then, after we recognize them, let us pray for the strength to act upon them while gratefully acknowledging His hand in our lives.

I love Jesus Christ, my Father in Heaven, and our living prophet. I support the Brethren in every way I can. I pray that this book may be a help to you and a reminder to me, and therefore a stepping-stone to more closely doing as God would have us do.

Selected Bibliography

Ball, Deanna and Terry, eds. *Each One a Miracle: Inspirational Romanian Adoption Stories*. Orem, UT: Grandin Book, 1994.

Bills, Diane. *Trust in the Lord*. American Fork, UT: Covenant Communications, Inc., 1996.

Burton, Rulon T. *We Believe—Doctrines and Principles of The Church of Jesus Christ of Latter-day Saints*. SLC: Tabernacle Books, 1994.

Cook, Gene R. *Receiving Answers to Our Prayers*. SLC: Deseret Book, 1996.

Garvin, Michele Romney, ed. *By Small and Simple Things*. American Fork, UT: Covenant Communications, Inc., 1996.

Goates, L. Brent. *Modern-Day Miracles*. American Fork, UT: Covenant Communications, Inc., 1996.